The Vegetarian Cookbook for a Keto Diet

Change Your Lifestyle and Stay Healthy with 750+ Simple Vegetarian Recipes from The Ketogenic Diet. Including a 28 Day Meal Plan to Take Control of Your Nutrition.

| *June 2021 Edition* |

© Copyright 2021 by Maria Smith

INTRODUCTION		**22**
KETO VEGETARIAN RECIPES		**27**
BREAKFAST		**27**
1.	Avocado with halloumi cheese	27
2.	Vegetarian pizza recipe	29
3.	Spinach lasagne with zucchini (9 servings)	31
4.	Keto rice with cheddar cheese (1 portion)	34
5.	Caprese (1 serving)	35
6.	Wege pasta (2 servings)	36
7.	Microwave Quick Keto Bread	38
8.	Pork cutlets	39
9.	Shakshuka with goat cheese	40
10.	Low Carb Chocolate Muffins	41
11.	Crispy Apple Pie with Zucchini	44
12.	Creamy Cucumber Sandwiches	46
13.	Coconut flour biscuits with cheese	48

14.	Breakfast in a cup with ham and cheese	50
15.	Zucchini Fritters	51
16.	Coconut flour biscuits with cheese	52
17.	Aerial keto waffles	53
18.	Keto omelet with minced meat	55
19.	Peanut Butter Pancakes	57
20.	Tuna Egg Rolls	58
21.	Waffle Chicken Sandwich	60
22.	Carrot Cream Muffins	64
23.	Chia Seed Pumpkin Pudding	66
24.	Matcha Chia Seed Pudding	67
25.	Pepperoni Cheese Muffins	68
26.	Cheese and Egg Tart	70
27.	Low carb muesli	71
28.	Low Carb Pizza Pie	72
29.	Garlic Cauliflower Fried Rice	75
30.	Bacon Egg Muffins	76
31.	Sausage Egg Casserole	77

32.	Simple Cream Cheese Pancakes	78
33.	Low carb egg noodles	79
34	Spinach Cheese Muffins	81
35	Fritters	83
36	Low Carb Chocolate Smoothie	85
37	Linen muffins for breakfast	86
38	Florentine Chicken Pancakes	88
39	Cheese Cookies	90
40	Low Carb Pancakes with Raspberries	91
41	Keto porridge grits	93
42	Mexican low carb breakfast	94
43	Cheesecakes with spinach	96
44	Low-Carbon Seed Bread	98
45	Almond Coconut Porridge with Berries	100
46	Low Carb Oatmeal	102
47	Keto Pancakes with Berries and Greek Yogurt	103
48.	Scrambled eggs with mushrooms and cottage cheese	105
49.	Keto cheesecakes	106

50.	Beef Muffins with Avocado and Cheese	107
51.	The Classic Bacon With Eggs	108
52.	Crispy Cheese Keto Omelette	110
53.	Ketogenic stuffed mushrooms	112
54.	Keto cured salmon with scrambled eggs and chives	114
55.	Keto fried eggs with kale and pork	115
56.	Omelet Caprese	117
57.	Scrambled eggs	119
58.	Keto eggs with avocado and bacon candles	120
59.	Ketogenic frittata of goat cheese and mushrooms	121
62.	Keto plate of turkey	123
63.	Omelet of keto cheese	124
64.	Coffee with cream	126
65.	Vegan Scrambled Eggs With Silk Tofu	127
66.	Warm Polenta Porridge With Fresh Fruits	129
67.	Oatmeal Breakfast Pizza	130
68.	Chocolate Chia Pudding With Warm Pear	132
69.	Cappuccino Waffles With A Kick	134

70.	Fluffy Protein Bread With Nutri-Plus	135
73.	Chia-Quinoa Breakfast	136
74.	Banana Chocolate Waffles	138
75.	Cappuccino Granola	139
76.	Blueberry Cheesecake	141
77.	Oatmeal-Banana Muffins	142
78.	Breakfast Couscous With Yoghurt, Cream And Fruits	144
79.	Breakfast - Fitness - Yogurt	146
80.	Smokeys cottage cheese and apple breakfast	147
81.	Warm apple and oatmeal porridge	148
82.	Yogurt - crunchy muesli with fruit salad	149
83.	Polenta semolina pudding with apple purée	150

LUNCH 151

84.	Microwave Quick Keto Bread	151
85.	Fried chicken with ginger	153
86.	Sharpened Lamb Shoulder (Keto)	154
87.	Keto Shepherd's Pie	156
88.	Moroccan meatballs in a slow cooker	158

89.	Salmon fillet with asparagus in hollandaise sauce	160
90.	Spinach Cheese Bread	162
91.	Soup with pork and fennel (in a slow cooker)	163
92.	Low Carb Shakshuka	164
93.	Chicken casserole with broccoli and cheese	166
94.	Spicy Pumpkin Casserole	168
95.	Cheese bread with bacon	169
96.	Chicken casserole with olives and feta cheese	171
97.	Low-Carb Meat Lasagna with Cheese	173
98.	Stuffed Pepper Keto Casserole	176
99.	Stuffed Pepper Keto Casserole	178
100.	Steak with Sliced Mushrooms	180
101.	Low Carb Garlic Mushrooms	182
102.	Cheeseburger Casserole with Bacon	183
103.	Simple low carb pizza	185
104.	Braised Beef with Noodles and Mushrooms	187
105.	Pork chops with tomatoes and mozzarella	189
106.	Low-carb beef and eggplant skewers	190

107.	Avocado Low Carb Burger	192
108.	Thai style pork roast with basil	194
109.	Chicken thighs in creamy tomato sauce	196
110.	Baked pork chops with a cheese crust	198
111.	Low carb beef roll	200
112.	Crispy Ginger Mackerel with Vegetables	202
113.	Spinach Egg Casserole	204
114.	Thai fried chicken with cashew nuts	206
115.	Low carb steaks with cauliflower puree	208
116.	Almond Noodles (Pasta)	210
117.	Chicken Breasts with White Sauce	212
118.	Creamy Pumpkin Muffins	214
119.	Shirataki noodles with cheese	216
120.	Crispy squash pie	218
121.	Low-Carbon Baked Beans with Beef	219
122.	Simple stew with beef stew	220
123.	Creamy Cheese Soup with Broccoli	220
124.	Green Bean Chicken Casserole	221

125.	Asparagus Stuffed Chicken Breasts	223
125.	Stuffed Tomatoes with Minced Meat and Cheese	224
126.	Crispy Bacon Chicken Pizza	226
127.	Low Carb Chicken Noodle Soup	228
128.	Low Carb Chicken Noodle Soup	230
129.	Creamy Salmon Soup with Coconut Milk	232
130.	Cabbage Puree with Bacon	234
131.	Low carb egg noodles	235
132.	Cheeseburger Low-Carb Pie	237
133.	Mushroom roll with nuts and spinach	239
134.	Meat muffins	241
135.	Jalapeno cheese biscuits	243
136.	Jalapeno Low Carb Bagels	244
137.	Cheeseburger Low Carb Casserole	246
138.	Frittata with caramelized onions and cabbage	248
139.	Focaccia Low Carb Bread	250
140.	Toasted Tofu with Peanut Sauce	252
141.	Delicious low-carb buns	254

142.	Creamy Cheese Soup with Broccoli	255
143.	Homemade bread with walnuts	256
144.	Homemade bread with rosemary and olives	258
145.	Low-Carbon Seed Bread	260
146.	Fish in tomato sauce	262
147.	Sea Bass and Peppers Salad	263
148.	Mexican baked beans and rice	265
149.	Easy Baked Shepherd Pie	266
150.	Fish in the herb, garlic, and tomato sauce	268
151.	Hot Salad with Kale and White Beans	270
152.	Scallion Swordfish	272
153.	Easy Zucchini Spaghetti	274
154.	Cauliflower Rice	276
155.	Salmon With Capers Sauce	277
156.	Bacon Cupcake	279
157.	Chicken With Okra	280
158.	Green Salad With Chicken	282
159.	Baked Eggplant	284

160.	Baked Fish Fillet	285
161.	Low Carb Chicken Quiche	287
162.	Baked Eggplant Salad	288
163.	Fish in tomato sauce	290
164.	Sea Bass and Peppers Salad	291
165.	Mexican baked beans and rice	293
166.	Easy Baked Shepherd Pie	295
167.	Fish in the herb, garlic, and tomato sauce	297
168.	Hot Salad with Kale and White Beans	299
169.	Scallion Swordfish	301
170.	Jambalaya Rice Recipe (also simply called Jambalaya)	303
171.	Chick Curry (Thai Chicken)	306
172.	Fried breaded lasagna with marinara sauce	308
173.	Baked Mushrooms with Pumpkin And Chipotle Polenta	310
174.	Cauliflower and Pumpkin Casserole	312
175.	Thai beef salad Tears of the Tiger	314
176.	Stuffed apples with shrimp	316
177.	A Quick Recipe of Grilled Chicken Salad with Oranges	318

178.	Red Curry with Vegetable	320
179.	Baked Turkey Breast with Cranberry Sauce	322
180.	Oatmeal and berry muffins	324
181.	Crunchy Blueberry and Apples	326
182.	Fresh Cranberry Pie	328
183.	Low carb chocolate mousse	330
184.	Chocolate Keto Cake with Peanut Butter Cream	332
185.	Low carb chocolate peanut squares	334
186.	Eggplant and chickpea bites	334
187.	Baba Ghanouj	337
188.	Spicy crab dip	338
189.	Potatoes" of Parmesan cheese	339
190.	Chili cheese chicken with crispy and delicious cabbage salad	340
191.	KETO pumpkin pie for Halloween, sweet and spicy	342

DINNER 344

192.	**Italian Keto Casserole**	**345**
193.	**Salmon Keto Cutlets**	**347**
194.	**Brussels sprouts with maple syrup**	**348**
195.	**Baked Cauliflower**	**349**
196.	**Mushroom Risotto with Mushrooms**	**351**
197.	**Low Carb Green Bean Casserole**	**352**
198.	**French Zucchini (Gratin)**	**354**
199.	**Avocado Low Carb Burger**	**355**
200.	**Italian sausages in a slow cooker with pepper**	**357**
201.	**Low carb goulash**	**357**

202.	Low carb egg noodles	359
203.	Baked ratatouille	361
204.	Avocado roll with a vegetable salad	363
205.	Baked salmon with a nut crust	365
206.	Ginger Pumpkin Soup	366
207.	Celery and Cauliflower Puree	367
208.	Braised cod in a tomato broth	368
209.	Benedict Salad with Bacon and Eggs	369
210.	Baked Eggs with Ham and Asparagus	371
211.	Cabbage Keto Cutlets	372
212.	French pie with mushrooms, spinach and goat cheese	373
213.	Creamy cheese soup with vegetables	375
214.	Creamy Spinach	377
215.	Cheese Halibut Cheese Bread	379
216.	Baked Eggplant with Cheese	380
217.	Shrimp with zucchini with alfredo sauce	382
218.	Keto mousaka with ground beef and zucchini	384
219.	Salmon fillet with vegetables	386

220.	Salmon fillet with cream sauce	388
221.	Keto Blue Casserole	390
222.	Salmon cutlets with parmesan	392
223.	Jalapeno Cheese Pizza	394
224.	Chile con carne	396
225.	Keto Chili	397
226.	Rutabaga and Cauliflower Patties	399
227.	Spicy Sausage and Pepper Soup	401
228.	Ham and cheese pie	403
229.	Shrimp and Cauliflower Curry	405
230.	Low Carb Chicken Stew	407
231.	Moroccan low-carb meatballs	408
232.	Casserole with bacon and cheese	410
233.	Stuffed Peppers Poblano	412
234.	Pepperoni Low Carb Pizza	413
235.	Miso Salmon	415
236.	Soup with red pepper and cauliflower	417
237.	Jalapeno Keto Soup	419

238.	Salmon with cream sauce	421
239.	Keto casserole with tuna	423
240.	Keto pizza in 5 minutes	425
241.	Bacon Keto Cheeseburger	426
242.	Pumpkin Keto Carbonara	427
243.	Hot Chili Keto Soup	429
244.	Zucchini noodles with avocado cream and tomatoes	431
245.	Vegan fitness kebab	433
246.	Gluten-free chickpea soup with Nutri-Plus Shape & Shake	434
247.	Protein gnocchi with basil pesto	436
248.	Vegan rosemary roulade with potatoes, broccoli and mushroom sauce	438
249.	Protein rice pudding	440
250.	Vegan sliced à la Bombay	441
251.	Summery bowls with fresh vegetables and protein quark	443
252.	Crispy asparagus tart with Nutri-Plus	445
253.	Protein-rich asparagus cream soup	447
254.	Meat and Kidney Pie	449

255.	Cauliflower and Pumpkin Casserole	451
256.	Thai beef salad Tears of the Tiger	453
257.	Stuffed apples with shrimp	455
258.	A Quick Recipe of Grilled Chicken Salad with Oranges	457
259.	Red Curry with Vegetable	459
260.	Baked Turkey Breast with Cranberry Sauce	461
261.	Parsnip soup, pear with smoked nuts	463
262.	Moroccan style chickpea soup	465
263.	Tuscan soup of chard and white beans	467
264.	Blueberry jam, grapes, and chia seeds	469
265.	Thick mushroom and wine sauce	470
266.	Stuffed mushroom heads	471
267.	Grilled Eggplant Sandwich	473
268.	Creamy Cucumber Dip	475
269.	Humus without oil	476
270.	Spiced carrot and white bean dip	477
271.	Cucumber and kale open sandwich	479
272.	Fried rice noodles with nut sauce and meatballs	480

273.	Spring pasta with sprouts	482
274.	Mushroom tofu with smoked tofu	483
275.	Asian tofu with soba noodles	484
276.	Marinated portobello steaks	486
277.	Chickpeas meatballs - like from a Swedish buffet	488
278.	Caldo Verde - Portuguese kale soup	490
279.	Tomato cream of red lentils	492
280.	Simple miso soup - for a cold!	494
281.	Warming cream of baked vegetables	496
282.	Watermelon gazpacho in a jar	498
283.	Mango soup with cider and chili	500
284.	Peanut sweet potato ginger cream	502
285.	Pumpkin spice syrup	504
286.	Matcha vegan cheesecake	505
287.	Vegan delicacies	507
288.	Christmas cocktail - vegan eggnog	509

VEGETABLE RECIPES 511

327. Boar stew with vegetables, herbs and plums, a Tuscan recipe 512

328. Turkish ACMA with sheep's cheese and vegetables 514

329. My creamy, vegan peanut fritters with vegetables and soy 516

330. Bolognese sauce with lots of vegetables 519

331. Vegetables - lasagna a la mouSse 521

332. Fried noodles with vegetables and meat (Asian) 523

333. Salmon with vegetables and potatoes 525

334. Fried salmon on Mediterranean vegetables 527

335. Oven Chicken With Vegetables 529

336. Beefsteak with mustard and herb topping and vegetables 531

ENTRIES 533

337. Eggplant and chickpea bites 533

338. Baba Ghanouj 535

339. Mixes of snacks 535

340. Herbal Cream Cheese Tartines 537

341. Spicy crab dip 538

342. Potatoes" of Parmesan cheese 540

343.	"Potatoes" cheese keto	541
344.	Low carb halloumi chips, with avocado sauce	542
345.	Low carb granola bars	544
346.	Keto "corn" fritters	546
347.	Tequeños low in carbohydrates	547

© Copyright 2021 by Maria Smith

All rights reserved. No part of this guide may be reproduced in any form without permission in writing from the publisher except in the case of brief quotations embodied in critical articles or reviews.

Legal & Disclaimer

The information contained in this book and its contents is not designed to replace or take the place of any form of medical or professional advice; and is not meant to replace the need for independent medical, financial, legal or other professional advice or services, as may be required. The content and information in this book have been provided for educational and entertainment purposes only.

The content and information contained in this book has been compiled from sources deemed reliable, and it is accurate to the best of the Author's knowledge, information and belief. However, the Author cannot guarantee its accuracy and validity and cannot be held liable for any errors and/or omissions. Further, changes are periodically made to this book as and when needed. Where appropriate and/or necessary, you must consult a professional (including but not limited to your doctor, attorney, financial advisor or such other professional advisor) before using any of the suggested remedies, techniques, or information in this book.

Upon using the contents and information contained in this book, you agree to hold harmless the Author from and against any damages, costs, and expenses, including any legal fees potentially resulting from the application of any of the information provided by this book. This disclaimer applies to any loss, damages or injury caused by the use and application, whether directly or indirectly, of any advice or information presented, whether for breach of contract, tort, negligence, personal injury, criminal intent, or under any other cause of action.

You agree to accept all risks of using the information presented inside this book.

You agree that by continuing to read this book, where appropriate and/or necessary, you shall consult a professional (including but not limited to your doctor, attorney, or financial advisor or such other advisor as needed) before using any of the suggested remedies, techniques, or information in this book.

INTRODUCTION

First, what is the ketogenic diet?

Next, let's see what is the basis of the ketogenic diet or keto. The main objective of the ketogenic diet is to burn more calories from healthy fats and proteins than from hydrates. When the diet is followed correctly, the body will enter a state called ketosis.

Some calorie burning takes place in the average person when the body breaks down hydrates or sugars. By focusing on increasing dietary fat and protein consumption and depriving the body of hydrates, you will start burning fat and protein and eventually experience greater weight loss.

Besides weight loss, it has been shown that in a number of diseases and medical problems the ketogenic diet improves symptoms.
Low-carbohydrate diets including keto have been shown to be effective in alleviating symptoms of diabetes, raising good cholesterol and even helping to treat neurological diseases including epilepsy.

Can the ketogenic diet be vegetarian?

The bottom line is that yes, the ketogenic diet is accessible to vegetarians. Although you have to work harder to ensure the right amount of protein, there is no reason for someone who does not eat animal protein to think that the keto diet is not for them.

"The conventional ketogenic diet can be extremely meat-based, not to mention that you can push back anyone who wishes to follow a more plant-based diet," says Dr. Will Cole of the Functional Medicine Certification Program, and Author of the Ketotarian plant-based ketogenic diet book.

A vegetarian ketogenic diet, on the other hand, has the advantages of eating a high-fat diet without the common inflammatory effects of conventionally processed meats.

"Fundamentally, a plant-based diet can reach greener eating habits and may have detoxification properties, help fight cancer, and also keep blood sugar under control," says Dr. Cole.

As we mentioned before, healthy fats are the holy grail when we talk about the keto diet. And the types of high-fat vegetarian foods are easy to find. The key is to be aware that following a keto vegetarian diet is a notable change from the starting point of the common vegetarian.

If you are a vegetarian who tends to substitute meat with alternatives full of hydrates such as pasta, bread and crackers, or lower sources of carbohydrates such as beans and lentils, then the transition may not be very smooth.

But ultimately, health compensation makes an effort worthwhile.

Keto vegetarian diet proteins

In people who carry an omnivorous diet many intakes are made up of meat and eggs, or fish-based dishes. However, these are not valid foods in a vegetarian diet.

Here then, the main sources of protein will be eggs and cheeses, as well as substitutes for meat with low carbohydrate intake, such as tofu or seitan for example.

Also, we will go to other sources of vegetable proteins that contain almost no hydrates, that is, we can consume seeds such as pumpkin or sunflower seeds, or nuts such as pistachios, cashews or nuts that are the options that have more protein concentrate.

Fats in the vegetarian keto diet

As we have said, in ketogenic diets, proteins and healthy fats must be simultaneously increased in order to reduce hydrates to less than 10% of daily calories.

Thus, the daily diet is based on protein foods such as those mentioned above and on sources of healthy fats such as various vegetable oils, mainly extra virgin olive oil; seeds and nuts, avocado, olives or capers.

Foods to avoid in the vegetarian ketogenic diet

For the ketogenic diet to work, that is, to produce ketosis, it is key to reduce hydrates and then, despite being a vegetarian diet, it cannot include cereals of any kind of foods that contain them, nor they admit sugars even in minimal quantities.

On the other hand, fruits and vegetables (except those mentioned above that are primarily fats) are not foods that can be consumed freely but are avoided as much as possible, especially those that have a higher concentration of sugar or hydrates.

Depending on the person you can eat some fruits and vegetables with low intake in hydrates such as citrus, green leaves, cucumber, celery or eggplant, but always in limited quantities since if we are not physically active we can easily leave the state of ketosis.

In addition, legumes that are a good source of vegetable protein cannot be included in the vegetarian diet, as they also provide hydrates that hinder the achievement of ketosis and thus prevent the keto diet from being properly carried out.

As you can see, the keto or ketogenic diet that is not easy to carry out is even more complex and limited if we are vegetarians, but proper planning can help us achieve it as we suggested before.

KETO VEGETARIAN RECIPES

BREAKFAST

1. Avocado with halloumi cheese

Ingredients:

- 1 avocado
- 140 g halloumi cheese
- 1 teaspoon butter for frying
- 1 tablespoon of olive oil
- 1/4 cup sour cream
- ¼ fresh cucumber
- 1 tbsp pistachio nuts
- salt and pepper
- ¼ lemon (optional)

Instructions:

- Halloumi cheese cut into slices, heat butter in a frying pan and fry the cheese until golden brown.
  - While the cheese is frying, cut the avocado and remove the stone.
- Cut the cucumbers into sticks and place with avocado on a plate - sprinkle with lemon juice, olive oil and sprinkle with salt and pepper.
- Serve with fried cheese and sour cream.
- If you don't like cucumber, you can easily replace it with another crunchy vegetable, e.g. celery, radish, kohlrabi.

2. **Vegetarian pizza recipe**

Cake Products:

- 2 eggs
- ½ cup mayonnaise
- ¾ cup of almond flour
- 1 tablespoon of plantain husk
- 1 teaspoon of baking powder
- ½ tsp salt

Products-Extras:

- 50-60 g mushrooms
- 1 tablespoon of green pesto
- 2 tablespoons of olive oil
- ½ cup 18% cream
- ¾ cup grated cheese
- salt and pepper
- arugula

Instructions:

- Preheat to 175 ° C in the oven.
- Combine well the eggs and mayonnaise, add to the dough the remaining ingredients, combine and wait for 5 minutes.
- Then add on your hands a few drops of oil and evenly spread the dough on a baking tray lined with baking paper. The thickness should be no more than 1 cm.
- Bake until the dough starts to brown lightly for 10 minutes. Clear from the oven and let it cool down. Cut the mushrooms in thin slices at this moment.
- Put the cream on the cooled cake and add oil and spices to the pesto.
- Sprinkle with the aged cheese and finish with the mushrooms. Place the pizza 5-10 minutes in the oven until the cheese is dissolved. Serve with salad from the rocket.

3. Spinach lasagne with zucchini (9 servings)

Ingredients :

- 4 medium courgettes
- 450 g mozzarella - crumbled
- 1 teaspoon parsley - chopped
- 1 tablespoon of olive oil
- ½ onions - finely chopped
- 4 garlic cloves - crushed
- 420 g ricotta
- 1 large egg
- ½ cup grated Parmesan cheese

- 2 tablespoons of tomato paste
- 1 can of tomatoes without skin
- Salt and black pepper to taste
- 1 tablespoon of fresh chopped basil
- 3 cups fresh spinach

Instructions:

- In a saucepan in olive oil, fry the onion, add garlic and fry - make sure that the garlic does not burn. Then add the tomato concentrate and chopped canned tomatoes mix well. Season with salt and pepper. Cook for 25-30 minutes on medium heat so that the sauce evaporates slightly. Finally, remove from heat and add fresh basil and spinach. Mix well.
- Heat the oven to 190 ° C. Cut zucchini into thin slices, slicing lengthwise - a potato peeler or sharp knife is great for this. Arrange the slices of zucchini in one layer on a baking tray lined with baking paper. Bake for 5-8 minutes. Remove from the oven, wait 5 minutes and drain the excess water with a paper towel. This part is very important so that lasagna is not watery.
- In a medium bowl, mix the ricotta cheese, parmesan cheese and egg well. Line the bottom of a 22x30cm ovenproof dish or baking dish with ⅓ tomato sauce and spinach, ⅓ zucchini slices, then ⅓ cheese mix and ⅓ grated mozzarella cheese.

- Perform the next 2 layers in the same way. There must be mozzarella on top. Cover the heat-resistant dish with aluminum foil and bake for 30 minutes. Then remove the foil and bake for another 10-15 minutes.
- Let stand for about 10 minutes before serving. Garnish with parsley.

4. Keto rice with cheddar cheese (1 portion)

Ingredient :

- 3 cups of grated cauliflower
- 1 cup grated broccoli
- 1 tablespoon of butter
- 1/2 teaspoon salt
- 1/4 teaspoon pepper
- 1/4 teaspoon garlic powder
- a pinch of ground nutmeg
- 1/2 cup shredded spicy cheddar cheese
- 1/4 cup mascarpone

Instructions:

- Grate cauliflower and broccoli on a grater put into a bowl and add salt, pepper, and garlic - mix well.
- Heat butter in a frying pan and pour the mixture, fry for about 6-8 minutes on medium heat, stirring.
- Then add cheddar cheese and fry for another 2-3 minutes, stirring.
- Combine it with mascarpone cheese to achieve a creamy consistency. Season according to your taste.
- Serve hot.

5. Caprese (1 serving)

Ingredients:

- 60 g cherry tomatoes
- 60 g mini mozzarella
- 1 teaspoon of green pesto
- salt and pepper

Instructions:

- Cut in half the tomatoes and balls of mozzarella. Add and whisk the pesto.
- To taste the salt and the pepper. New basil or chopped parsley can be added.

6. Wege pasta (2 servings)

Ingredient :

- 4 eggs
- 150 g Philadelphia cream cheese
- ½ tsp salt
- 40 ml (20 g) of ground ovoid husk

Sauce

- 100 g Blue Blue cheese
- 100 g Philadelphia cream cheese
- 30 g butter
- 1 pinch of pepper

For serving

- 2 tablespoons of roasted nuts
- 60 ml freshly grated Parmesan cheese

Instructions:

- Preheat the oven to 150 ° C.

- Mix the eggs, cheese, and salt into a liquid dough. Continue mixing by adding plantain husk. Let the dough rest for 2 minutes.
- Place the dough on a parchment paper-lined baking sheet. Use a rolling pin to put another parchment on top and flatten it.
- Place the parchment cake in the oven and bake for 10-12 minutes. Heat the paper and cut it.
- Cut the pasta with a pizza cutter or a sharp knife into thin strips. Place in the refrigerator.
- Until serving, refresh the pasta: heat the pasta in a microwave or oven sauce for 30 seconds. Melt the blue cheese gently over low heat in a small saucepan, stirring periodically.
- Apply cream cheese and, for a few minutes, blend well.
- Remove butter and mix it together. Don't put to a boil the sauce.
- Use the noodles to eat. Top with freshly grated Parmesan cheese and roasted nuts.

7. Microwave Quick Keto Bread

Ingredients:

- 3 tbsp almond flour
- ½ tsp psyllium powder
- ½ tsp baking powder
- A pinch of salt
- 1 tbsp ghee
- 1 large egg

Instructions:

- Add the dry ingredients to a small bowl, then butter and egg. Mix well.
- Lubricate the microwave, mug, or small bowl, and add the batter.
- Put the bread in the microwave for 80-100 seconds.
- Gently place the bread on a cutting board and cut in half.

8. Pork cutlets

Ingredients:

- 450 g minced pork
- 1 tsp ground sage
- 1 tsp dried rosemary
- 1 tsp salt
- 1 tsp ground pepper
- ¼ tsp ground fennel
- ⅛ tsp chili powder
- 1 tbsp olive oil for frying

Instructions:

- Mix in a bowl all the ingredients except the oil.
- Divide the mixture into 6 balls and form cutlets.
- Pour oil into a large frying pan with a non-stick coating over high heat and fry the patties for 2-3 minutes on each side until cooked.

9. Shakshuka with goat cheese

Ingredients

- ¼ cup olive oil
- 3 cups chopped greens
- 1 medium yellow onion, diced
- 1 medium jalapeno chopped
- ½ medium green bell pepper, diced

- 4 garlic cloves, minced
- 1 tbsp paprika
- ½ tsp chopped red pepper
- Salt and pepper to taste
- 800 g sugar-free tomato puree
- 6 large eggs
- 113 g goat cheese

Instructions:

- Preheat the oven to 204 degrees. Heat the pan over medium heat and heat the olive oil.
- Once it is hot, add herbs, onions, jalapenos, green bell peppers, and garlic. Cook everything until soft, then add paprika, chopped red pepper, salt, and black pepper.
- Add the tomato puree and continue cooking until the sauce is pleasant and hot. Turn off the fire.
- Using a spoon, make holes in the sauce, then break into each egg.
- Put the pan in the oven and bake for 5 minutes.
- Top crumble the goat cheese.

10. Low Carb Chocolate Muffins

Ingredients:

- 226.8 g almond flour
- 0.03 kg coconut flour
- 2 tsp baking powder
- A pinch of salt
- 113.4 g unsalted butter (melted)
- ⅓ cup stevia
- 1 tsp vanilla essence
- 2 large eggs
- ⅓ cups of chocolate drops without sugar (minimum 80% cocoa). Or you can just grind low-carb chocolate.

Instructions:

- Preheat the oven to 180 degrees. Layout the baking sheet with parchment paper.
- Combine almond and coconut flour, baking powder and salt.
- Beat with a mixer the oil, sweetener, and vanilla essence for 5-8 minutes, until light and fluffy. Add one egg at a time and then flour. Mix well.
- Add chocolate and whisk again.
- Put the dough on a piece of parchment paper and squeeze it into a circle about 2.5 cm thick.
- Cut like a pizza into 8 slices. Gently peel the slices with a spatula or knife.

- Bake for 15-20 minutes until the buns begin to brown. When pressed to the center, they should be a little soft.
- Leave on a baking sheet for 10 minutes.

11. Crispy Apple Pie with Zucchini

Ingredients:

The foundation:

- 744 g peeled and chopped zucchini
- 3 tbsp lemon juice
- 121.33 g low carbohydrate sugar substitute
- 0.75 tsp ground cinnamon
- 0.5 tsp ground nutmeg

- 1 tsp apple extract (optional)

Filling:

- 49.5 g chopped pecans
- 56 g almond flour
- 30 g oat fiber or coconut flour
- 45.5 g low carbohydrate or erythritol sugar substitute
- 1 tsp cinnamon
- 56.75 g butter

Instructions:

- in a medium bowl, combine zucchini, lemon juice, sweetener, cinnamon, and nutmeg until smooth. To enhance the apple flavor, add apple extract. Pour the mixture into a greased 9 x 9-inch baking dish.
- Combine the pecans, almond flour, oat fiber, sweetener and cinnamon in a bowl, then cut the butter into cubes and mix. Sprinkle with zucchini mixture.
- Bake at 176 degrees for 45-50 minutes or until the zucchini is soft.

12. Creamy Cucumber Sandwiches

Ingredients:

- 85 g cream cheese
- 1 medium cucumber
- 1 tbsp sour cream
- 1/8 tsp salt
- 1 pinch of pepper
- 1/8 tsp garlic powder
- Almond flour bread or other low-carb bread

Instructions:

- Grate the cucumber and let the excess liquid drain.
- Mix cream cheese, cucumber, and sour cream until smooth. Season with salt, pepper and garlic powder.
- Cut the slices of low-carb bread in half to make them thinner. Put the cucumber mixture on the bottom slice and cover it with the top slice. Cut in half.

13. Coconut flour biscuits with cheese

Ingredients

- 4 eggs
- 56.75 g melted butter
- 0.25 tsp salt
- 2 tsp garlic powder
- 0.25 tsp onion powder
- 40 g coconut flour
- 0.5 tsp xanthan gum (optional)
- 0.25 tsp baking powder
- 56.5 g chopped cheddar cheese

Cooking

- Beat eggs, oil, salt, garlic, and onion powder together.
- In a separate bowl, mix coconut flour with baking powder and xanthan gum.
- Add the dry ingredients to the egg mixture. Beat and add cheese.
- Place the dough with a tablespoon on a greased baking sheet.
- Bake at 204 degrees for 15 minutes.

14. Breakfast in a cup with ham and cheese

Ingredients:

- 12 slices of ham
- 4 eggs
- 1 tbsp grated parmesan cheese
- 1 tbsp chopped parsley
- 1 tsp olive oil for lubrication
- 1/4 tsp sea salt
- 1/4 tsp black pepper

Instructions:

- Preheat the oven to 176 degrees.
- Divide 12 slices of ham between 4 muffin or ramekin molds (greased with olive oil).
- Break each egg into each pan, season with salt and pepper, and bake for 20 minutes.
- Serve immediately, sprinkled with parmesan and chopped parsley

15. Zucchini Fritters

Ingredients:

- 226.8 g chopped chicken
- 1 zucchini
- 28 g almond flour
- 1 beaten egg
- 56.7 g grated gouda cheese
- 1 tbsp fresh chopped dill
- 1 ½ tbsp olive oil for frying
- Salt and pepper to taste

Instructions:

- Grate the zucchini, put in a bowl, sprinkle with a pinch of salt and mix well. Let stand for at least 10 minutes.
- Transfer to cheesecloth or a kitchen towel, and squeeze the water well.
- Put in a bowl and add chopped chicken, beaten egg, almond flour, cheese, dill, season with salt and pepper, and mix well.
- Form pancakes to your taste (in this recipe 6 pcs.).
- Heat the oil in a frying pan over medium heat and fry the pancakes for 3-4 minutes on each side or until tender.
- Put on a plate and serve with leafy greens, aioli or any other low-carb sauce to your taste.

16. Coconut flour biscuits with cheese

Ingredients:

- 4 eggs
- 56.75 g melted butter
- 0.25 tsp salt
- 2 tsp garlic powder
- 0.25 tsp onion powder
- 40 g coconut flour
- 0.5 tsp xanthan gum (optional)
- 0.25 tsp baking powder
- 56.5 g chopped cheddar cheese

Instructions:

- Beat eggs, oil, salt, garlic, and onion powder together.
- In a separate bowl, mix coconut flour with baking powder and xanthan gum.
- Add the dry ingredients to the egg mixture. Beat and add cheese.
- Place the dough with a tablespoon on a greased baking sheet.
- Bake at 204 degrees for 15 minutes.

17. Aerial keto waffles

Ingredients:

- 1 1/2 cup almond flour
- 2 tbsp coconut flour
- 1/2 tsp baking powder
- 1 tsp baking soda
- 2 large whole eggs
- 1 tbsp maple extract
- 2 tbsp stevia or another low-carb sweetener
- 2 tbsp melted butter
- 1 1/4 cup unsweetened milk to your taste

Instructions:

- Put all the ingredients in a large bowl. Mix well with a spatula or mixer until smooth. Leave on for 5 minutes.
- Preheat the waffle iron and grease with a non-stick spray, butter or coconut oil.
- Pour the dough into waffle iron and cook for 3-4 minutes until golden on each side. Place the finished waffles in the oven so that they are crispy while you cook the remaining waffles.

- For the topping, try homemade almond butter, cream cheese, and strawberries, or whipped coconut cream.

18. Keto omelet with minced meat

Ingredients:

- 85.05 g pork or ground beef
- 2 eggs
- 1 tbsp fat cream
- 1 tsp hot low carb sauce
- 2 tbsp cheddar cheese
- 2 tsp olive oil (individually)
- Sea salt and pepper to taste
- 1 tsp chopped green onions

Instructions:

- Break the eggs into a blender. Pour in heavy cream, and season with salt and pepper. Mix everything together until smooth.
- Heat 1 teaspoon of olive oil in a pan, add the minced meat and cook for 5 minutes or until brown.
- Add hot sauce, season with salt and pepper, and cook another 1-2 minutes. Set aside.
- Place the pan over medium heat and pour the remaining olive oil. When the oil is warm, carefully pour the beaten eggs into the pan, cover and leave until cooked.

- After the omelet is fried, put the minced meat on one side, sprinkle with chopped cheese, and then roll the omelet.
- Cover and cook over low heat for another 1-2 minutes until the cheese melts.
- Transfer to a dish and sprinkle with chopped green onions.

19. Peanut Butter Pancakes

Ingredients:

- 1 1/4 cup peanut flour
- 2 tsp stevia or erythritis
- 1 tbsp baking powder
- 1/2 tsp salt
- 1 1/2 cup unsweetened almond or coconut milk
- 2 eggs
- 1/4 cup natural peanut butter
- 1 tsp vanilla extract

Instructions:

- In a medium bowl, mix dry ingredients. In a separate bowl, mix the wet ingredients until smooth.
- Add wet ingredients to dry ingredients and beat until batter forms. If the dough is too thick, add milk.
- Put 1 tablespoon in a heated pan, and brown until brown on both sides.

20. Tuna Egg Rolls

Ingredients:

- 2 eggs
- 1 tbsp fat cream
- 79.38 g canned tuna canned (drained)
- ¼ chopped avocado
- 12 g lettuce
- 2 tbsp low carb mayonnaise (separate)
- 1 tsp chopped dill
- 1 tsp lemon juice
- Sea salt and black pepper to taste
- 1 tsp butter

Instructions:

- Break the eggs into a blender. Pour in heavy cream, and season with salt and pepper. Mix everything together until smooth.
- Melt a teaspoon of oil in a medium pan. Gently pour the beaten eggs, cover and fry until tender.
- Mix tuna, mayonnaise, dill and lemon juice in a bowl. Add salt and pepper and mix well.
- Place the omelet on a plate and brush with mayonnaise. Layout a mixture of tuna, sliced avocado, and lettuce.

- Roll up the omelet so that the filling is inside. Halve and serve warm with your favorite low-carb sauce.

21. Waffle Chicken Sandwich

Ingredients:

Waffles:

- 2 tbsp ghee
- 3 large eggs, protein separated from yolks
- 1/4 cup milk
- 1 cup almond flour
- 1/2 tsp salt
- 1 tsp vanilla
- 1 tbsp erythritis

A hen:

- 1 cup buttermilk (nonfat cream)
- 2 medium chicken breasts
- 1 large egg
- Olive oil for frying
- Salt and pepper to taste
- 1 tsp paprika
- 1/4 tsp cayenne powder
- Additionally: maple syrup without sugar, bacon, pickles and mustard.

Instructions:

- Cut the chicken breasts in half lengthwise. Cut these slices in half lengthwise, four strips into the chicken breast. Soak the buttermilk strips overnight.
- Remove the chicken from buttermilk, then season with salt, pepper, cayenne powder and paprika.
- In a bowl, beat the egg, then set the bowl aside. In a separate bowl, combine almond flour, as well as a little salt and pepper. Lubricate each piece of chicken with an egg, then with almond flour. Grease each slice again with an egg and then with almond flour so that there are two layers of breading.
- Heat a little olive oil in a pan, then quickly cook both sides of each chicken stripe so that it is fried outside. Put each piece of chicken on a baking sheet and cover with foil. Bake at 176 degrees for 15 minutes or until tender.
- Preheat the waffle iron. Beat egg yolks, milk, erythritol, ghee, and vanilla together. Beat almond flour and salt until lumpy.
- Beat the egg whites with a hand mixer until the foam is formed. Gently pour the eggs into the waffle dough, half at a time.
- Lubricate the waffle iron, then add 1/3 cup servings of dough and cook each wafer for 5-6 minutes or until brown.
- Serve wafers with chicken on top and mustard. Put a piece of bacon and two cucumbers on each wafer, then cover the sandwich with another waffle and sprinkle with sugar-free

maple syrup. Poke a toothpick so that the sandwich does not fall apart before serving.

22. Carrot Cream Muffins

Ingredients:

- 4 eggs (protein separated from yolks)
- 1 tsp greasy whipped cream
- 50 g of powdered erythritol
- 0.25 tsp stevia powder extract
- 56 g almond flour
- 60 g oat fiber
- 96 g carrots
- 0.5 tsp baking powder
- 62.5 g almond milk
- 56 g butter
- 1 tsp allspice
- 1 tsp cinnamon
- 24.75 g chopped pecans

Filling:

- 226.8 g cream cheese
- 1 egg
- 1 tbsp coconut flour
- 50 g of powdered erythritol
- 0.25 tsp stevia powder extract

- 0.5 tsp vanilla extract

Instructions:

- Beat egg white and cream until foamy.
- In a separate bowl, combine egg yolks, erythritol, stevia, almond flour, oat fiber, almond milk, butter, allspice, cinnamon and carrots until smooth.
- Gently add egg white and pecans.
- Pour the batter into a well-greased muffin pan.

Filling:

- Beat cream cheese with egg, coconut flour, 1/4 cup erythritol, 1/4 teaspoon of stevia and 1/2 teaspoon of vanilla until a homogeneous mass is formed.
- Put a couple of teaspoons of the toppings on each muffin.
- Bake at 176 degrees for 20-25 minutes.

23. Chia Seed Pumpkin Pudding

Ingredients:

- 339 g coconut milk or unsweetened almond milk
- 184 g pumpkin puree
- 12 drops of liquid stevia
- 1 tsp vanilla extract
- 0.5 tsp cinnamon
- 0.25 tsp ground ginger
- 0.25 tsp nutmeg
- 0.13 tsp carnations
- 42.5 g chia seeds

Instructions:

- Beat milk, pumpkin, vanilla, and spices together. Add chia seeds and mix.
- Refrigerate for a couple of hours or overnight.

24. Matcha Chia Seed Pudding

Ingredients:

- 4 matcha green tea bags
- 83.33 ml of boiling water
- 45.5 g low carbohydrate sweetener
- 437.5 ml unsweetened almond or coconut milk
- 56.67 g chia seeds

Instructions:

- Brew green tea for about 3-5 minutes. Take out the bags.
- Add sweetener, almond milk and chia seeds to brewed tea. Mix well.
- Continue stirring every 5 minutes for 15 minutes.
- Serve and cool.

25. Pepperoni Cheese Muffins

Ingredients:

- 141.75 g cream cheese
- 50 g minced Parmesan cheese
- 30 g coconut flour
- 74.67 g almond flour
- 1 tsp baking powder
- 0.5 tsp salt
- 3 tbsp water
- 5 beaten eggs
- 56.5 g mini pepperoni
- 112 g chopped mozzarella

Instructions:

- Preheat the oven to 204 ° C. Lubricate the muffin tins.
- In a large bowl, combine cream cheese, grated Parmesan cheese, almond and coconut flour, baking powder, salt, water, and beaten eggs.
- Add pepperoni and 1/2 cup mozzarella cheese.
- Fill the muffin molds 1/2 to 3/4.
- Top with 1/2 cup mozzarella cheese.

- Bake for 25-30 minutes, or until the muffins are firm and lightly browned.

26. Cheese and Egg Tart

Ingredients:

- 227 g grated cheddar cheese
- 12 large eggs
- 114 g soft cream cheese
- 12 tablespoons unsalted melted butter
- Salt and pepper to taste

Instructions:

- Put about half the cheese in a 9.5-inch cake pan.
- Add eggs and cream cheese to a food processor or blender.
- Beat eggs and cream cheese by slowly adding melted butter.
- Pour the egg mixture onto the cheese in a baking pan.
- Sprinkle the remaining grated cheese on top.
- Bake at 162 °C for 45 minutes.
- Remove from the oven and cool on the wire rack for several minutes before slicing.
- Store leftovers in the refrigerator (about a week) or in the freezer (for a longer period).

27. Low carb muesli

Ingredients:

- 134 g of sunflower seeds
- 85 g unsweetened coconut
- 64 g pumpkin seeds
- 143 g chopped almonds
- 49.5 g pecans
- 100 g hemp seeds
- 2 tsp cinnamon
- 0.5 tsp vanilla extract
- 0.25 tsp liquid stevia

Instructions:

- Thoroughly mix all the ingredients in a large bowl.
- Place on a baking tray and bake at a temperature of 176 degrees for about 7-8 minutes.
- Let cool. Store in an airtight container.
- Each serving is about 1/3 cup. It goes well with almond milk!

28. Low Carb Pizza Pie

Ingredients:

Dough:

- 1 ½ cup almond flour
- ¼ cup coconut flour
- 1 tsp salt
- 6 tbsp diced cold butter
- 1 tsp xanthan gum
- 1 tsp vinegar
- 1 large egg

Filling:

- 15 slices of pepperoni
- 6 large eggs whipped together
- 1 cup oily whipped cream

- 1 cup grated mozzarella
- Salt and pepper to taste
- ½ tsp Italian seasoning
- ¼ tsp red pepper

Instructions:

- Add almond flour, coconut flour, salt, xanthan gum, and vinegar to the food processor. Beat several times, then add the cold butter. Continue whipping until the dough for the cake looks like bread crumbs. Add the beaten egg and beat again until the dough has gathered in a ball. Wrap with plastic wrap and refrigerate for 45-60 minutes.
- Preheat the oven to 176 degrees. Grease a baking sheet and a piece of foil with a non-stick spray then set aside.
- When the dough has cooled, place it between two sheets of parchment paper. Roll the dough into a circle of about 25 cm. If you want to make a lot of pies, roll out more circles. Remove the top layer of parchment and transfer the dough into a cake pan; if the dough crumbles, knead it with your fingers.
- Pour the egg mixture into the pie, covering with pepperoni and cheese. Sprinkle with the remaining cheese.
- Add half of mozzarella and pepperoni inside with a uniform layer. Then mix the eggs, milk, Italian seasoning, chopped red pepper, salt, and black pepper in a bowl.

- Cover with foil and bake for about 35-45 minutes. Remove the foil and continue baking for another 15 minutes.

29. Garlic Cauliflower Fried Rice

Ingredients:

- 3 tbsp olive oil
- 3-4 minced garlic cloves
- 480 g cooked cauliflower
- 3 eggs whipped with a fork (optional)
- 2 tbsp unsweetened almond milk
- 3 slices of ham or bacon
- 1 tbsp soy sauce
- Chopped onion (optional)

Instructions:

- Heat the olive oil over medium heat in a large skillet.
- Add the garlic (and chopped onions when using) and simmer until the garlic begins to brown.
- Add the cauliflower and mix, then slide aside.
- Mix eggs and almond milk, then pour onto another pan and fry the omelet.
- Add scrambled eggs to cauliflower and mix. Add the ham.
- Mix with soy sauce and stir over medium heat for a minute or two until everything is warm.

30. Bacon Egg Muffins

Ingredients:

- 12 slices of bacon
- 12 large eggs
- 226 g grated cheddar cheese

Instructions:

- Bake bacon in the oven at 204 ° C for 10-12 minutes. Take it out before it becomes crispy.
- Sprinkle cupcake tins (12 pcs.) With a non-stick spray. Layout each bacon pan.
- Beat the eggs and add the grated cheese.
- Spread the mixture over the tins.
- Bake for about 25 minutes at 176 ° C.

31. Sausage Egg Casserole

Ingredients:

- 455 g of beef sausage or sausages
- 226 g coconut milk
- 224 g grated cheese (cheddar or mozzarella)
- 6 large eggs
- Salt and pepper to taste

Instructions:

- Fry chopped sausage or sausages in a pan until brown.
- Beat eggs and coconut milk. Season with salt and pepper.
- Lubricate the 8 x 8-inch baking tray with non-stick spray. Pour a thin layer of egg mixture, spread the ground sausage on top. Sprinkle with grated cheese. Pour the rest of the egg mixture evenly.
- Bake at 176 degrees for about 20-30 minutes.

32. Simple Cream Cheese Pancakes

Ingredients:

- 113 g soft cream cheese
- 4 large eggs
- 2 tsp stevia or erythritis
- ½ tsp vanilla extract
- 1 tbsp butter (for greasing the pan)

Instructions:

- Put cream cheese, eggs, sweetener, and vanilla extract in a high-speed blender. Mix well until smooth.
- Heat a large non-stick pan over low heat. Melt ¼ teaspoon of butter on it.
- Pour 1/4 cup of dough into the pan. Cover and cook for 2 minutes on each side until golden brown. Repeat step with remaining batter.
- Add sugarless maple syrup, butter or coconut oil, etc. if desired.

33. Low carb egg noodles

Ingredients:

- 3 egg yolks
- 113.4 g soft cream cheese
- 0.13 tsp garlic powder fresh grated Parmesan cheese (about 1/3 cup plus 2 tablespoons)
- 37.33 g of freshly grated mozzarella cheese (about 1/3 cup plus 2 tablespoons)
- 0.13 tsp dried basil
- 0.13 tsp dried marjoram
- 0.13 tsp dried tarragon
- 0.13 tsp ground oregano
- 0.13 tsp ground black pepper

Instructions:

- Beat egg yolks and cream cheese together. Add the parmesan and mozzarella, and continue whisking. Sprinkle with spices and beat well again.
- Put a baking sheet on parchment, and evenly distribute the cheese-egg mixture on it. Smooth with a spatula or the back of a spoon.
- Place the pan in the preheated oven to 246 ° C and reduce the temperature to 176 ° C.
- Bake 5 to 8 minutes. If small bubbles begin to appear, reduce the temperature to 148 ° C and continue to bake for 2-3 minutes until cooked.
- Let cool at room temperature for 10 to 15 minutes. Slice with a regular pizza knife or knife.

34 Spinach Cheese Muffins

Ingredients:

- 90 g cooked spinach
- 38 g coconut flour
- 4 eggs
- 56 g unsalted butter (melted)
- 4 chopped green onions
- 75 g crumbled feta cheese
- 25 g grated Parmesan cheese
- 1 grated zucchini
- 1/2 tsp baking powder
- 1/4 cup water
- 1/4 tsp salt
- 1/4 tsp black pepper
- 1/2 tsp nutmeg
- 4 tbsp chopped fresh parsley

Instructions:

- Preheat the oven to 200 degrees.

- Beat eggs, oil, water, and salt with a hand blender or whisk.
- Add coconut flour and baking soda, and mix well.
- Add green onions, zucchini, spinach, parsley, and nutmeg. Mix well.
- Add feta cheese and parmesan, and mix. Season with salt and pepper.
- If the mixture is too thick, add more water (approximately ¼ cup).
- Place the dough in a muffin dish.
- Bake for 20-25 minutes until golden brown.

35 Fritters

Ingredients:

- 354.37 g white fish (3 medium filets)
- 2 chopped onions
- A small piece of fresh ginger (about 2.5 cm), peeled and chopped
- 3 chili or jalapenos
- 1 beaten egg
- 4.93 g garlic powder
- 2.46 g dried thyme
- 29.57 g coconut flour
- 59.15 g of olive oil
- 2.46 g of salt

Instructions:

- Put the fish fillet in the microwave for 2 minutes. Then mash it with a fork.
- Add green onions, ginger, chili pepper, garlic powder, salt, and thyme. Mix well.
- Add beaten egg and coconut flour, and mix again.
- Form small pancakes (about 10 pieces).
- Heat the olive oil in a pan over medium heat.

- Gently fry the fish pancakes for about 2-3 minutes, until golden brown on both sides.

36 Low Carb Chocolate Smoothie

Ingredients:

- 28 g dark chocolate (minimum 80% cocoa)
- 2 tbsp peeled hemp seeds
- 2 tbsp erythritis
- 1 tbsp cocoa powder
- 1/2 cup chilled coconut cream
- 1/2 medium avocado
- 1/2 cup almond milk
- 1 glass of ice

Instructions:

- Grind the chocolate in a powerful blender, then add cocoa powder, sweetener and hemp seeds, and beat well.
- Add remaining ingredients and beat until smooth

37 Linen muffins for breakfast

Ingredients:

- 160 g ground flaxseed
- 112 g almond flour
- 100 g low carbohydrate erythritol
- 4.93 g of baking powder
- 1.23 g of salt
- 4.93 g nutmeg
- 14.79 g of cinnamon
- 113.5 g unsalted butter
- 4 beaten eggs

Topping (optional):

- 29.57 g unsalted butter
- 4.93 g of cinnamon
-

Instructions:

- Heat the oven to 180 degrees.
- Combine all dry ingredients together.
- Add beaten eggs and melted butter to the dry mixture, and mix well. If the mixture is a little thick, add about 1/4 cup of water.

- Fill out the muffin forms with a little more than half the dough.
- Bake for 20 minutes until the tops are golden brown. Cool on a baking sheet for several minutes.
- Mix extra cinnamon and melted butter, then dip the tops of the muffins (optional)

38 Florentine Chicken Pancakes

Ingredients:

- 4 almond pancakes (see recipe)
- 1 boneless skinless chicken breast
- 3/4 cup fresh spinach
- 2 tbsp greasy whipped cream
- 50 g grated Parmesan cheese
- 113 g grated mozzarella cheese
- 56 g butter
- 1/2 tbsp garlic powder
- 1/2 tsp salt
- 1/2 tsp black pepper

Instructions:

- Heat the oven to 180 degrees.
- Heat oil in a frying pan over medium heat.
- Cut the chicken into small pieces and cook in a pan for about 7 minutes until cooked.
- Add spinach and cook another 2 minutes.
- Add seasoning, Parmesan cream cheese, and half Mozzarella. Stir until the cheese melts, then remove from heat.

- Put the pancakes on the kitchen board and spread the mixture. Gently roll the pancakes and put them in a greased pan.
- Sprinkle the second half of Mozzarella cheese.
- Bake for 15 minutes until the cheese melts.

39 Cheese Cookies

Ingredients:

- 230 g grated cheddar cheese
- 60 g butter, melted and slightly chilled
- 4 eggs
- 80 g coconut flour
- 1/4 tsp baking powder
- 1/4 tsp garlic powder
- 1 tsp dried parsley (optional)
- 1/4 tsp salt

Instructions:

- Preheat the oven to 200 ° C.
- Break the eggs into a bowl. Add garlic powder, melted butter, and dried parsley. Salt to taste.
- Add cheese, baking powder, and coconut flour to the mixture. Mix well until lumps remain in the mixture.
- Oil the baking sheet, then form 8 cookies and bake for 15 minutes.

40 Low Carb Pancakes with Raspberries

Ingredients:

- ½ cup almond flour
- ½ cup coconut flour
- 2 tbsp keto sweetener
- 4 large eggs
- ¼ cup unsweetened almond milk or coconut milk
- ¼ cup fresh raspberries
- A pinch of salt

Instructions:

- Mix all the ingredients until a thick dough is formed. Leave on for 5 minutes.
- Heat a large non-stick pan over low heat.
- Pour 1/4 cup of dough into the pan, and cook for 2-3 minutes on each side until the edges turn golden brown.

41 Keto porridge grits

Ingredients:

- 2 cups cauliflower
- 1/4 tsp garlic powder
- 1/2 tsp salt
- 1/4 tsp pepper
- 1/4 cup hemp hearts
- 2 tbsp butter
- 56 g grated cheddar cheese
- 1/4 cup fat cream
- 1 cup unsweetened milk of your choice

Instructions:

- Melt the butter in a cast-iron skillet over low heat.
- Add chopped cauliflower and hemp hearts, and fry for two minutes.
- Add heavy cream, milk, garlic powder, salt, and pepper. Stir well and simmer until the mixture thickens and the cauliflower is soft. Add more milk or water as needed.
- Remove from heat and add cheddar cheese.

42 Mexican low carb breakfast

Ingredients:

Filling:

- 2 eggs
- 1/4 chopped onion
- 113 g minced chicken
- ½ chopped jalapeno peppers
- 1/8 tsp garlic powder
- 1/2 tsp ground caraway seeds
- 1/4 cup low-carb salsa
- 1 ½ tbsp olive oil
- Salt and black pepper to taste

Cakes:

- 1/2 cup cheddar cheese
- 1/2 cup grated mozzarella

Stuffing (optional):

- 28 g feta cheese
- 1 tablespoon fresh chopped cilantro

Instructions:

- Fry the chopped onion in heated oil for about 2 minutes to make it soft. Add minced chicken and jalapenos, and stir for 3-4 minutes. Season with salt and pepper, ground caraway seeds, garlic powder, and salsa. Reduce heat and leave the pan for 6–8 minutes.
- In another non-stick pan, fry the eggs in half a tablespoon of oil.
- Combine mozzarella and cheddar in a small bowl, and mix well. Divide the mixture into 2 parts, and fry in a pan with cheese for 2-3 minutes. Let the cheese melt before serving.
- Put on the cheesecakes the previously prepared filling. Add the egg, feta cheese, and salsa, and sprinkle with cilantro before serving.

43 Cheesecakes with spinach

Ingredients:

- 2 eggs
- 30 g fresh chopped spinach
- 75 g crumbled feta cheese
- 2 chopped green onions
- 1 clove garlic, chopped
- 112 g almond flour
- 2.46 g of baking powder
- 1.23 g nutmeg (optional, but tasty!)
- 2.46 g of salt
- 2.46 g black pepper
- 62.5 g of water
- 29.57 g unsalted frying butter

Instructions:

- Beat the eggs until foamy.
- Add almond flour, baking powder, and water, and beat until smooth.
- Add spinach, chives, garlic, feta cheese and mix well.
- Season with nutmeg, salt, and pepper.
- Heat the butter in a pan over medium heat.

- Put a few tablespoons of dough in a frying pan and form cheesecakes from them.
- Cook on each side until golden brown.

44 Low-Carbon Seed Bread

Ingredients

- 33.5 g of sunflower seeds
- 16 g pumpkin seeds
- 14.79 g chia seeds
- 60 g coconut flour
- 29.57 g of flax flour
- 2 eggs
- 4 egg whites
- 29.57 g coconut oil
- 14.79 g of baking powder
- 29.57 g of psyllium powder
- 14.79 g apple cider vinegar
- 2.46 g of salt
- 125 g boiling water

Instructions:

- Preheat the oven to 180 degrees.
- Lubricate and lay out the base of the bread pan with a strip of parchment paper.
- Combine coconut flour, psyllium powder, baking powder, salt, flax flour, sunflower seeds, pumpkin seeds, chia seeds in a

bowl (leave a couple of tablespoons of pumpkin and sunflower seeds to sprinkle).
- Add eggs and mix thoroughly.
- Add oil and mix until smooth and slightly sticky.
- Add apple cider vinegar and stir. The dough may bubble and change color due to the chemical reaction of vinegar, do not be alarmed!
- Add a little water until you get a texture that looks like dough.
- Pour the mixture into a bread pan, smoothing it evenly.
- Sprinkle the remaining seeds on top.
- Bake for 30 to 35 minutes.

45 Almond Coconut Porridge with Berries

Ingredients:

- 2 tbsp ground flaxseed
- 1 tbsp almond flour
- 1 tbsp unsweetened coconut
- ½ teaspoon vanilla powder
- ½ tsp cinnamon
- 1/3 cup coconut milk
- ½ cup almond milk
- 1/4 cup berries
- 1 tsp dried pumpkin seeds

Instructions:

- Heat the pan on the stove. Add flaxseed, almond flour, coconut, vanilla powder, cinnamon, coconut and almond milk to the pan.
- Heat the pan over medium heat, stirring constantly, until the mixture becomes hot and thickens (it will resemble oatmeal).
- Pour the porridge into a bowl, and add the berries and pumpkin seeds.

Low Carb Oatmeal

Ingredients:

- 1 cup unsweetened almond or coconut milk
- 1 scoop MCT powder
- 1 tsp cinnamon
- 1/2 cup hemp seed
- 1 tbsp Flaxseed
- 1 tbsp chia seed
- 1 tbsp coconut flakes

Instructsions:

- Combine all the ingredients in a small saucepan, and put on low heat, stirring occasionally. Remove from heat when the mixture thickens.
- Transfer to a bowl, and add frozen berries and nuts.

47 Keto Pancakes with Berries and Greek Yogurt

Ingredients:

- 4 eggs
- 226 g cream cheese
- 56 g butter
- 1/4 tsp sugar-free cranberry extract
- 1 tsp cocoa
- 1 cup greek yogurt
- Wild berries for decoration (optional)
- Frying oil

Instructions:

- Combine the butter and eggs in a large bowl, and beat for two minutes.
- Now add cream cheese, cranberry extract and cocoa.
- Continue whisking until smooth for three minutes.
- Lubricate a small nonstick pan with a little oil and heat over medium heat. Add about three tablespoons of the mixture and cook for two minutes on each side.
- Remove from heat and place one tablespoon of Greek yogurt on top. Garnish with wild berries if desired.

48. Scrambled eggs with mushrooms and cottage cheese

Ingredients:

- 4 eggs
- 226 g cream cheese
- 56 g butter
- 1/4 tsp sugar-free cranberry extract
- 1 tsp cocoa
- 1 cup greek yogurt
- Wild berries for decoration (optional)
- Frying oil

Instructions:

- Heat olive oil in a large skillet.
- Fry finely chopped onion in butter until it becomes clear.
- Add the chopped mushrooms and simmer until the liquid in the pan evaporates. Mix well with oregano, pepper and salt. Set aside.
- Beat the eggs and season with pepper and salt. Fry in a pan and mix with a wooden spoon.
- Put the scrambled eggs on a dish with mushrooms and cottage cheese.

49. Keto cheesecakes

Ingredients:

- 450 g cream cheese
- 1 cup coconut flour
- 2 eggs
- A pinch of salt to taste, optional
- 1 tsp Stevia to taste, optional

Instructions:

- Combine cream cheese, coconut flour, salt and 2 eggs.
- Form cheesecakes and sprinkle a little coconut flour.
- Fry until both sides are golden brown.
- Serve with blueberries or other keto filling to your taste.

50. Beef Muffins with Avocado and Cheese

Ingredients:

- 1 kg of ground beef
- 10 medium-sized eggs
- 1/2 cup fat cream
- 2 avocado cubes
- 280 g diced cheddar cheese
- Black pepper to taste

Instructions:

- Preheat the oven to 176 ° C.
- Take a large cupcake pan and place the ground beef on them, pressing it to the bottom and walls.
- Spread avocados and cheese evenly into shapes.
- Beat the eggs and cream, then pour the mixture into each pan and season with black pepper.
- Bake for 20 minutes.

51. The Classic Bacon With Eggs

It is one of the best ketogenic breakfasts that exist! Make this classic something even more delicious with this beautiful recipe. Enjoy the number of eggs you need to satisfy yourself, depending on your level of hunger. Just thinking of this keto dish makes our mouths water!

Ingredients

- 8 eggs
- 150 g bacon, sliced
- cherry tomato (optional)
- fresh parsley (optional)

Instructions

- Fry the bacon until it is crispy. Set aside on a plate.
- Fry the eggs in the bacon fat the way you like it. Cut the cherry tomatoes in half and fry them at the same time.
- Salpimentar to taste.

52. Crispy Cheese Keto Omelette

Once you've tried this omelet, there will be no going back. Its irresistible crust and sumptuous filling will make it your favorite omelet. It is ideal for a good breakfast, but it is also a great option for a quick keto dinner .

Ingredients

Omelet

- 2 eggs
- 2 tbsp whipping cream
- salt and ground black pepper
- 1 tbsp butter or coconut oil
- 75 g grated or sliced cheese, cured

Filling

- 2 sliced mushrooms
- 2 sliced cherry tomatoes
- 2 tbsp (30 g) cream cheese
- 15 g spinach sprouts
- 30 g turkey cold cuts
- 1 tsp dried oregano

Instructions

- In a bowl, beat the eggs, cream, salt, and pepper.

- Heat a tablespoon of butter in a nonstick skillet over medium heat. Spread the cheese evenly in the pan so that it covers the entire bottom. Fry over medium heat until bubbly.
- Carefully incorporate the egg mixture over the cheese and reduce heat — Cook a few minutes without stirring.
- Fill half with mushrooms, tomatoes, spinach, cream cheese, turkey, and oregano — Fry a few more minutes.
- When the egg mixture begins to set (it can still be quite loose on top, but not too much), turn the empty half over half with the ingredients, forming a half-moon. Fry a few more minutes and enjoy!

53. Ketogenic stuffed mushrooms

This dish is super simple and versatile. You can serve these tasty ketogenic snacks on a large plate as an appetizer, or they can be a side dish for your favorite food. No matter how you do it, prepare yourself for an indulgence that is as rich as it is healthy.

Ingredients

- 12 mushrooms
- 225 g bacon
- 2 tbsp Butter
- 200 g (200 ml) cream cheese
- 3 tbsp fresh chives, finely chopped
- 1 tsp Spanish paprika
- salt and pepper

Instructions:

- Preheat the oven to 200 ° C.
- Stir in the bacon until crisp. Allow to cool and process to crumble. Save fat from the bacon
- Remove the stalk from the mushroom and chop finely. Stir in the fat and add butter if necessary.

- Put mushrooms in an oiled frying pan.
- In a bowl, crushed bacon with fried mushroom stalk and mix the remaining ingredients. Fill each mushroom with a small amount of mixture.
- Bake for 20 minutes or until the mushrooms are brown.

54. Keto cured salmon with scrambled eggs and chives

Breakfast superstars shine with their own light on this simple meal. Scrambled eggs seasoned perfectly with a tasty garnish of apple-cured salmon; A nutritious breakfast the sea easy! Get ready to beat, and then eat!

Ingredients

- 2 eggs
- 2 tbsp Butter
- 60 ml whipping cream
- 1 tbsp fresh chives, chopped
- 50 g cured salmon
- salt and pepper

Instructions

- Beat the eggs well. Melt the butter in a pan. Add the cream and heat carefully while stirring.
- Simmer the mixture for a few minutes while constantly stirring so that the eggs are creamy.
- Season with chopped chives, salt, and freshly ground pepper. Serve with several slices of cured salmon .

55. Keto fried eggs with kale and pork

Present something delicious! The eggs and vegetables, along with the crunchy nuts and the crispy pork, give you great texture and flavor. Create this wonder keto loaded with butter in a single pan any night of the week!

Ingredients

- 225 g kale
- 75 g butter
- 175 g smoked pork bacon or bacon
- 60 ml frozen blueberries
- 30 g (75 ml) pecans or nuts
- 4 eggs
- salt and pepper

Instructions

- Cut and chop the kale into large squares (pre-washed kale is an excellent shortcut). Melt two-thirds of the butter in a pan and fry the kale quickly over high heat until it browns a little around the edges.
- Remove the kale from the pan and set aside. Brown the bacon or pork bacon in the same pan until they are crispy.
- Lower the heat. Put the sauteed kale back in the pan and add the blueberries and nuts. Stir until hot — Reserve in a bowl.

- Raise the heat and fry the eggs in the rest of the butter. Salpimentar to taste place two fried eggs with each serving of vegetables and serve immediately.

56. Omelet Caprese

Ingredients

- 2 tbsp olive oil
- 6 eggs
- 100 g cherry tomatoes, cut in halves or tomatoes cut into slices
- 1 tbsp fresh basil or dried basil
- 150 g (325 ml) fresh mozzarella cheese
- salt and pepper

Instructions

1. Break the eggs in a bowl to mix and add salt and black pepper to taste. Beat well with a fork until everything is completely mixed. Add basil and stir.
2. Cut the tomatoes into halves or slices. Chop or slice the cheese.

3. Heat the oil in a large skillet. Fry the tomatoes for a few minutes.
4. Pour the egg mixture over the tomatoes. Wait until it becomes a little firm and add the cheese.
5. Lower the heat and let the omelet harden. Serve immediately, and enjoy!

57. Scrambled eggs

Ingredients

- 2 eggs
- 30 g butter
- Salt and ground black pepper

Instructions

1. Beat the eggs together with some salt and pepper using a fork.
2. Melt the butter in a nonstick skillet over medium heat. Look closely: butter does not turn golden!
3. Pour the eggs into the pan and mix for 1-2 minutes until they are creamy and cooked a little less than you like. Remember that the eggs will continue to cook even once you put them on your plate.

58. Keto eggs with avocado and bacon candles

Ingredients

- 2 eggs, hard
- ½ avocado
- 1 tsp olive oil
- 60 g bacon
- salt and pepper

Instructions

1. Preheat the oven to 180 ° C (350 ° F).
2. Put the eggs in a pot and cover with water. Bring to a boil and let simmer for 8-10 minutes. Place the eggs in ice water as soon as they are made to make it easier to peel them.
3. Split the eggs into two halves along and take out the yolks. Put them in a small bowl.
4. Add avocado and oil to the bowl and mash until mixed. Salt and pepper to taste.
5. Place the bacon in a baking sheet and bake until crispy. Take 5-7 minutes. You can also fry them in a pan.
6. With a spoon, carefully add the mixture to the egg whites and place the bacon candle. To enjoy!

59. Ketogenic frittata of goat cheese and mushrooms

Ingredients

- Frittata
- 150 g mushrooms
- 75 g fresh spinach
- 50 g chives
- 50 g butter
- 6 eggs
- 110 g goat cheese
- Salt and ground black pepper
- At your service
- 150 g green leafy vegetables
- 2 tbsp olive oil
- Salt and ground black pepper

Instructions

1. Preheat the oven to 175 ° C (350 ° F).
2. Grate or crumble the cheese and mix in a bowl with the eggs. Salt and pepper to taste.
3. Cut the mushrooms into small pieces. Chop the chives.
4. Melt the butter over medium heat in a pan suitable for the oven and fry the mushrooms and onions for 5-10 minutes or until golden brown.

5. Add the spinach to the pan and fry for another 1-2 minutes. Pepper.
6. Pour the egg mixture in the pan. Bake for about 20 minutes or until browned and firm in the middle.
7. Serve with green leafy vegetables and olive oil.

62. Keto plate of turkey

Ingredients

- 175 g turkey cold cuts
- 2 avocados
- 75 g (75 ml) cream cheese
- 50 g lettuce
- 60 ml of olive oil
- Salt or pepper

Instructions

1. Put the turkey, sliced avocado, lettuce and cream cheese on a plate.
2. Pour olive oil over the vegetables and season to taste.

63. Omelet of keto cheese

Ingredients

- 75 g butter
- 6 eggs
- 200 g shredded cheddar cheese
- Salt and black pepper ground to taste

Instructions

1. Beat the eggs until soft and lightly frothy. Add half of the grated cheddar cheese and mix. Salt and pepper to taste.
2. Melt the butter in a hot pan. Pour the egg mixture and let stand for a few minutes.

3. Lower the heat and continue cooking until the egg mixture is almost done. Add the remaining grated cheese. Fold and serve immediately.

64. Coffee with cream

Ingredients

- 180 ml coffee, prepared the way you like
- 60 ml whipping cream

Instructions

1. Prepare the coffee as you like. Pour the cream in a small saucepan and heat gently while stirring until frothy.
2. Pour the hot cream into a large cup, add the coffee and stir. Serve at the moment as it is or with a handful of nuts or a piece of cheese.

65. Vegan Scrambled Eggs With Silk Tofu

Ingredients

- 300 g   silken tofu
- 100 g   Tofu, tight
- 30 g   Nutri-Plus Protein Powder Neutral
- 1 small one   onion
- A good pinch Kala namak
- Something   Salt, pepper, turmeric
- Fresh chives
- 1-2 tbsp neutral vegetable oil

Preparation

Preparation time: 20 minutes

1. Put the silk tofu, the protein powder, turmeric, Kala Namak, salt and pepper together in a blender jar and mix well with the blender.
2. Now crumb the firm tofu, cut the onion into small cubes and put them under the silk tofu mixture.
3. Heat some oil in a pan and add the mass for the vegan scrambled egg.
4. Slowly set it to a medium level and stir again and again.

5. Give the scrambled eggs, some time, it takes a little longer than the original! But the wait is worth it.
6. Once the desired consistency is achieved, you can fold in some fresh chives and enjoy your vegan scrambled eggs.

66. Warm Polenta Porridge With Fresh Fruits

Ingredients

- 250 ml of soy milk
- 50 g   polenta
- 30 g   Nutri-Plus Shape & Shake Vanilla
- 30 g   blueberries
- 1 kiwi
- 20 g   walnuts

Preparation

Preparation time: 15 minutes

1. Heat 150 ml of the soymilk in a small saucepan and stir the other 100 ml together with the protein powder.
2. Once the soy milk cooks, add polenta and protein mix and stir well.
3. Let it all swell for about 10 minutes and then you can already have breakfast.
4. Cut down the fruit and nuts of your choice and serve it with the polenta porridge.

67. Oatmeal Breakfast Pizza

Ingredients

- 50 g oatmeal
- 15 g   Nutri-Plus protein powder chocolate
- 1/2 tsp cinnamon
- 100 g   Soy yogurt, unsweetened
- Something fresh fruit of your choice
- Ripe banana

Preparation

Preparation time: 20 minutes including baking time

1. Peel a banana and crush it to a pulp with a fork.
2. Now add the oatmeal, the protein powder and some cinnamon.
3. Preheat the oven to 150 ° C and spread the dough in a circle on a baking sheet lined with baking paper.
4. Leave the dough in the oven for about 10-12 minutes and then cool down a bit so that you can easily remove it from the baking paper.
5. In the meantime, you can cut your favorite fruit smell.
6. Distribute the soya yogurt on the oatmeal pizza and top it with the fruit and other toppings of your choice.

Note: The nutritional values given here are calculated without the topping.

68. Chocolate Chia Pudding With Warm Pear

Ingredients

- 200 ml Plant drink (soy)
- 20 g   Nutri-Plus Shape & Shake Chocolate
- 15 g   Chia seeds
- 1 pear
- 5 g coconut oil
- something   Vanilla and cinnamon

Preparation

Preparation time: 10 minutes plus cooling time

At best, prepare this recipe the night before, so that the Chiapudding can swell in peace.

1. Put the plant drink in a blender jar and add the Shape & Shake protein powder.
2. Mix both together vigorously until no lumps are left.
3. Now add the Chia seeds and stir them, so they can swell in peace. Stir in the first hour between times, so that everything spreads well and the shake can be taken anywhere from the Chia seeds.
4. Leave the chi pudding in the fridge overnight.
5. Cut the pear down and heat some coconut oil in a small pot.

6. Add the pieces of pear to the pot and let it simmer for 2-3 minutes. Vanilla and cinnamon to it and already the pears to Chia pudding.

69. Cappuccino Waffles With A Kick

Ingredients

- 140g Flour
- 60g Nutri-Plus protein powder cappuccino
- 300ml soy milk
- 50ml espresso
- 2 tbsp Sunflower oil
- 1 pinch salt

Preparation

Preparation time: 20 minutes

The recipe is enough for 4 waffles

1. Put all the dry ingredients in a bowl and mix with each other.
2. Add the soymilk and the espresso.
3. Mix all ingredients quickly to a smooth dough.
4. Heat the waffle iron in front of us with some baking spray. Alternatively, you can brush it with margarine.
5. Put one trowel of dough per waffle into the waffle iron.
6. Bake and enjoy it.

70. Fluffy Protein Bread With Nutri-Plus

Ingredients

- 90 g   neutral Nutri-Plus protein powder
- 200 g   Cashews
- 200 g   linseed
- 500 g   Unsweetened soya yogurt
- 150 ml of water
- 100 g   Sunflower seeds
- 1 pck. baking powder
- 1/2 tsp salt

Preparation

Preparation time: 90 minutes

1. First put the cashews, linseed and protein powder in a blender and chop everything together to a coarse flour.
2. Then pour the soy yogurt, water, baking soda and salt into a bowl and add the cashew protein powder mixture.
3. Third Stir everything into a smooth dough and fill it into a baking paper-lined form.
4. Let the dough shell for about 10-15 minutes. In time, you can preheat the oven to 175 ° C.
5. Bake the bread for about 60 minutes. To make sure it's really baked through, do the stick test.
6. Allow cooling, to taste delicious and then let taste.

73. Chia-Quinoa Breakfast

1 servings

Ingredients

- 150 ml Almond milk
- 15 g   Chia seeds
- 50 g   quinoa
- 15 g   Nutri-Plus protein powder vanilla
- 1 msp vanilla
- 1/4 tsp cinnamon
- 50 g   raspberries

Preparation

Preparation time: 20 minutes

1. Rinse the quinoa thoroughly warm and simmer in a little water for about 15-20 minutes.
2. Chia seeds, vanilla, cinnamon, vanilla protein powder and almond milk in a shaker and mix vigorously until the protein powder has dissolved well.
3. Let quinoa cool and then add to the Chia-almond milk mixture.
4. Let it soak overnight in the fridge and enjoy in the morning with fresh berries.

74. Banana Chocolate Waffles

Ingredients

- 80 g   spelled flour
- 30 g   Nutri-Plus protein powder chocolate
- 10 g   xylitol
- 1 mature banana
- 1 g cinnamon
- 2 g vanilla
- 1 pinch salt
- 200 ml Almond milk, unsweetened

Preparation

Preparation time: 15 min

1. Fill all dry ingredients together in a high blender jar.
2. Peel the banana and add it in small pieces to the ingredients.
3. Now fill in the almond mixture and mix everything with the magic wand until a smooth dough is formed.
4. Heat up the waffle maker and add 2-3 tbsp of batter per waffle in the waffle iron.
5. Bake for a short time and then enjoy with a topping of your choice.

75. Cappuccino Granola

Ingredients

- 200 g   oatmeal
- 100 g   Nutmeg (cashew)
- 60 g   Nutri Plus protein powder cappuccino
- 40 g   coconut oil
- 30 g   agave nectar
- 30 g   linseed
- 1 teaspoon   cinnamon
- 1 pinch salt

Preparation

Preparation time: 15 minutes

- Preheat the oven to 140 ° C.
- Heat the nutmeg, coconut oil and agave syrup together in a small saucepan until a liquid mass is obtained.
- Third Then put all the dry ingredients together in a bowl.
- Mix the toasted ingredients thoroughly and then add the liquid mass.
- Now you mix everything together and spread it on a baking sheet lined with baking paper.

- Put the granola in the oven for about 30-45 minutes to dry. Make sure it is not too dark, if necessary, lower the temperature slightly.
- Remove the finished granola from the oven and allow it to cool completely.
- Bottling and enjoy as needed.

76. Blueberry Cheesecake

Ingredients

- 80 g oatmeal
- 1 banana
- 100 ml oat milk
- 2 Teaspoons baking powder
- 20 g Nutri-Plus pea rice protein chocolate
- 150 g Vegan Quark
- 2 tbsp Blueberry pudding powder
- 1 teaspoon Erythritol (sugar replacement)
- 20 g blueberries

Preparation

Preparation time: 30 minutes

- Puree the banana with the milk and add the remaining dry ingredients and fill in a silicone mold.
- For the cheesecake cream, mix the quark with the custard powder and spread on the dough.
- Finally, distribute the blueberries on the cake.
- The cake must now bake at 200 ° C for about 20 minutes and cool overnight.

77. Oatmeal-Banana Muffins

Ingredients

- 50 g   Oatmeal, delicate
- 100 g   Spelled flakes or whole-grain flakes, ground
- 15 g   Spelled flour or whole-meal flour
- 1   Egg (he) (size M)
- 1 protein
- 1 / 2 Glass   Milk, low-fat (0.3 or 1.5%)
- 2 Teaspoons   olive oil
- 2 Banana (s), very ripe
- 7g baking powder
- Something   Honey, maybe
- paper cases

Preparation

Working time: approx. 15 minutes / cooking / baking time: approx. 40 minutes / difficulty level: simple

1. First, mix the spelled or whole-grain flakes into flour. Purée the bananas and add the eggs and milk. Blend these ingredients with the hand mixer until they mix well.
2. Then mix the flour with the baking powder. Now add all the remaining ingredients to the dough and mix again until everything has mixed well. If you want the muffins extra

sweet, you can also add honey, but I have prepared them without honey and after baking at breakfast with honey or jam eaten.

3. Pour the dough into a muffin tin filled with paper cups and push the mold into the oven on the middle rail. Bake the muffins at 180 ° C top / bottom heat for about 40 min and stick a toothpick into the muffins to see if they are done. You could need up to 50 minutes of baking time.

78. Breakfast Couscous With Yoghurt, Cream And Fruits

Ingredients

- 50 g couscous
- 110 ml Milk, cooking
- 150 g Yogurt, low in fat
- 1 teaspoon linseed
- 1 teaspoon Chia seeds
- Something cinnamon
- Possibly. Almonds
- Fruit of choice, z. B. Mango

Preparation

Working hours: approx. 15 min. / Cooking / Baking time: approx. 3 min. Rest period: approx. 10 min. / Difficulty level: simple

1. Cover the couscous with boiling or very hot milk, cover and let stand for about 10 minutes. After 5 minutes, stir once so that the couscous is nice and easy.
2. In the meantime, combine yogurt with linseeds, Chia seeds and a little cinnamon (also known as almonds). Cut fruits of your choice.

3. Then pour the couscous into a container or a glass, add the yogurt, cream and finish with fruit.
4. A few Chia seeds, flax seeds and almond slivers can also be sprinkled over as decoration-

79. Breakfast - Fitness - Yogurt

Ingredients

- 150 g   Natural yoghurt
- 1 / 2   Apple
- 1 / 2   Banana (s)
- 20 g   oatmeal
- 20 g   cereal
- 1 teaspoon   honey

Preparation

Working time: approx. 5 min. / Difficulty level: simple / calorie p. P .: about 417 kcal

1. Cut apple and banana into pieces. Mix with yogurt, oatmeal and cereal. Sweet with honey to taste.

80. Smokeys cottage cheese and apple breakfast

Ingredients

- 200 g   cottage cheese
- 1 big one   Apple
- 2 tbsp   applesauce
- 1 tsp.   Ground cinnamon
- 1 tbsp   Walnuts, chopped

Preparation

Working time: approx. 10 min. / Difficulty level: simple

1. Core the apple, but do not peel, cut into small cubes and mix with the applesauce, cinnamon and nuts under the cottage cheese.

81. Warm apple and oatmeal porridge

Ingredients

- 30 g oatmeal
- 1 Apple
- 1 teaspoon sweetener
- 1 teaspoon ground cinnamon
- 150 ml of water

Preparation

Working time: approx. 10 min. / Difficulty level: simple / calorie p. P .: about 180 kcal

1. Put the oats together with the water, sweetener and cinnamon in a microwaveable dish. Cut the apple into small pieces and mix. The whole thing then for about 2 minutes at 600 Watt in the microwave. Enjoy warm.

82. Yogurt - crunchy muesli with fruit salad

Ingredients

- 300 g   Natural yogurt
- 1 tbsp honey
- 4 tbsp oatmeal
- 6 tbsp Muesli (crunchy muesli or cornflakes)
- 1 tbsp Walnuts, chopped
- 400 g   Fruits, fresh, seasonal
- 1 teaspoon lemon juice
- 2 tbsp orange juice

Preparation

Working time: approx. 10 min. / Difficulty level: simple

1. Beat the yogurt with honey until smooth, then mix in oatmeal, muesli or cornflakes and nuts.
2. For the fruit salad, wash the fruits, peel them if necessary and cut into pieces, drizzle with lemon and orange juice and mix well.
3. Fill the muesli in serving bowls and add the fruit salad.

83. Polenta semolina pudding with apple purée

Ingredients

- 250 ml Milk, low fat (1.5% fat)
- 30 g polenta
- 100 g   Applesauce or apple pulp or other fruit pulp
- Possibly. Fruit, cut small
- Possibly. nuts
- Possibly. desiccated coconut
- sweetener

Preparation

Working time: approx. 5 min. / Difficulty level: simple

- Bring the milk to a boil. Remove from heat, stir in the polenta and bring to a boil again. When it is thickened (goes very fast), remove from heat and stir in sweetener and apple pie.
- Now any fruit (I advise of pineapple and kiwi because of the acid) and nuts on top of it.

LUNCH

84. Microwave Quick Keto Bread

Ingredients

- 3 tbsp almond flour
- ½ tsp psyllium powder
- ½ tsp baking powder
- A pinch of salt
- tbsp ghee
- 1 large egg

Cooking

- Add the dry ingredients to a small bowl, then butter and egg. Mix well.
- Lubricate the microwave, mug, or small bowl, and add the batter.
- Put the bread in the microwave for 80-100 seconds.
- Gently place the bread on a cutting board and cut in half.

85. Fried chicken with ginger

Ingredients

- 2 tbsp oils
- 2 cloves of garlic
- medium green bell pepper, peeled and cut into strips
- 1 tbsp finely chopped fresh ginger
- 400 g boiled chicken
- 1 tbsp coconut amino acids
- ½ tsp salt

Cooking

- Heat the oil in a pan, and fry the garlic, pepper, and ginger for 1 minute.
- Add chicken and cook another 2 minutes.
- Add amino acids and salt, and fry for another 30 seconds.

86. Sharpened Lamb Shoulder (Keto)

Ingredients

- 3 tbsp olive oil
- 4 minced cloves of garlic
- tbsp dried mint
- tsp ground cinnamon
- tsp ground caraway seeds
- tsp salt
- ½ tsp ground chili
- Lemon zest and 1 lemon juice
- Lamb shoulder (about 1.8 kg)

Cooking

- In a small bowl, put all the ingredients except lamb. Mix well.
- Make deep cuts across the lamb's shoulder and rub it with the cooked marinade.
- Refrigerate for at least 4 hours, preferably at night.
- Preheat the oven to 150 degrees.
- Put the lamb on a large roasting pan and cook for 5-5.5 hours, covering it with aluminum foil after the first hour. Cook until the meat exfoliates from the bone.
- Remove from the oven and let stand for 20 minutes.

- Cut into slices and serve hot along with mashed cauliflower and low-carb sauce.

87. Keto Shepherd's Pie

Ingredients

- 2 tbsp butter
- 450 g minced lamb
- ½ medium yellow onion, chopped
- 3 minced garlic cloves
- ½ cup minced celery
- 2 tbsp sugar-free tomato paste
- 1 tbsp Worcestershire sauce
- ½ cup chicken stock
- ¼ cup dry red wine
- ½ tsp xanthan gum
- 680 g "cauliflower" rice
- 1 cup oily whipped cream
- 1 cup grated cheddar cheese
- ¼ cup grated parmesan
- 1 tsp dried thyme

Cooking

- Preheat the oven to 176 degrees. Heat oil in a large skillet.
- Put minced meat, onion, garlic, celery, tomato paste, Worcestershire sauce, red wine and chicken stock in a pan.

- Cook until the meat is lightly browned and the vegetables soft. Sprinkle with xanthan gum and mix.
- Put cauliflower rice, greasy whipped cream, cheddar cheese, parmesan and thyme in a food processor. Mix until cauliflower turns into a smoothie.
- Put the meat mixture in a baking dish, and on top lay the mashed cauliflower.
- Bake the cake for 45 minutes or until it is browned on top. Let cool for 10 minutes and serve.

88. Moroccan meatballs in a slow cooker

Ingredients

- 900 g ground beef
- small onion (grated)
- 4 minced cloves of garlic
- 1 large egg
- tbsp finely chopped cilantro
- 1 tbsp ground caraway seeds
- 1 tbsp ground coriander
- 1 tbsp ground smoked paprika
- tsp ground ginger
- 1 tsp ground cinnamon
- 1 tsp salt
- 2 tbsp olive oil
- 2 tbsp sugar-free tomato paste
- 1 ½ cup sugar-free tomato puree
- ½ cup beef broth
- ⅓ cup cilantro

Cooking

- In a large bowl, combine ground beef, half grated onion, half garlic, egg, cilantro, cumin, coriander, paprika, ginger, cinnamon, and salt.

- Form 2 tablespoons the size of a tablespoon and set aside. I got 40 pcs.
- Add the oil, remaining onion and garlic to a non-stick pan over high heat. Fry for 3-5 minutes until fragrant.
- Add tomato paste and cook for another 3 minutes. Put in a slow cooker, and add tomato puree and broth. Mix well.
- Add meatballs and cook over low heat for 5 hours.
- Mix with cilantro and serve with mashed cauliflower.

89. Salmon fillet with asparagus in hollandaise sauce

Ingredients

- tbsp avocado oil
- salmon fillets (about 113 g)
- 226 g asparagus
- 6 tbsp butter
- large egg yolks
- 1 tbsp fresh lemon juice
- Water if needed

Seasoning to taste:

- Salt
- Pepper
- Cayenne pepper
- Garlic powder
- Onion powder
- Paprika

Cooking

- Heat a cast-iron skillet over medium heat. Add avocado oil and let it warm. Season the salmon fillet with salt and pepper while you wait.

- Fry the salmon fillet with the skin down for 5 minutes or so. Turn the salmon filet over, then add the asparagus pods and cook for another 5 minutes.
- Heat the butter in a small saucepan, then removes from heat.
- Add the egg yolks to the blender along with salt, pepper, cayenne pepper, garlic and onion powder, and paprika. Beat for a few seconds, then open the top of the lid and slowly add oil while continuing to whisk. The mass should turn into Dutch sauce. If it is too thick, feel free to dilute it with a small amount of water.
- Serve salmon and asparagus with hollandaise sauce sprinkled on top.

90. Spinach Cheese Bread

Ingredients

- 225 g almond flour
- 2 tsp baking powder
- ½ tsp salt
- 100 g soft butter
- 85 g fresh spinach, chopped
- clove garlic, finely chopped
- 1 tbsp chopped rosemary
- large eggs
- 140 g grated cheddar cheese

Cooking

- Preheat the oven to 200 degrees.
- Put the almond flour, baking powder and salt in a large bowl. Mix well, then add oil and mix again.
- Add the remaining ingredients (if you wish, you can leave a little cheddar for the top of the bread). Mix well.
- Put the dough in a cast-iron skillet, greased with oil, and form a pancake with a thickness of about 3.5-4 cm.
- Bake for 25-30 minutes; then leave the bread in the pan for 15 minutes to cool.

91. Soup with pork and fennel (in a slow cooker)

Recipe

- 450 g pork neck
- 450 g of cauliflower chopped into flowers
- 280 g sliced fresh fennel
- 2 cloves of garlic, chopped into quarters
- tsp salt
- ½ tsp ground white pepper
- cups of water
- cup chicken stock
- 1 cup of fat cream

Cooking

- Put all the ingredients except the cream in a slow cooker.
- Cook at high temperature for 6 hours.
- Remove the pork from the soup and chop. Set aside.
- Beat the soup with a blender until smooth.
- Add cream and minced pork. Try it and, if necessary, add extra salt and pepper.

92. Low Carb Shakshuka

Recipe

- tbsp avocado oil
- 2 red bell peppers diced
- ½ medium yellow onion, chopped
- 3 cups chopped cabbage
- 2 tsp seasoning harissa
- 2 tsp garlic powder
- 2 tsp caraway seeds
- ½ tsp sea salt
- 2 tbsp low carb tomato paste
- 2 tbsp water
- 4 large eggs

Cooking

- Heat the avocado oil in a large skillet over medium heat.
- Add bell peppers and white onions, and sauté for 5 minutes.
- Add cabbage and spices, then tomato paste and water, stirring until smooth. Cook for another 5 minutes, then reduce heat.
- Make four recesses with a spoon and break into each egg. Sprinkle with salt and cook under the lid for 5 minutes or until the eggs are ready.

- Divide into four servings, put a keto-friendly spicy sauce on top and serve.

93. Chicken casserole with broccoli and cheese

Recipe

- 680.39 g boneless chicken breast
- 2 tbsp olive oil
- 2 tbsp butter
- 3 cloves of garlic
- tbsp dried chopped onions
- Salt and pepper to taste
- 0.5 teaspoon tarragon
- 184.27 g pickled mushrooms
- 120 g of white culinary wine or a few tablespoons of lemon juice
- 226.8 g cream cheese
- g sour cream
- 235 g chicken bone broth
- 453.59 g broccoli flowers
- 50 g parmesan cheese

Cooking

- Cut the chicken into small pieces.
- Fry the chicken with garlic and onions in olive and butter until the meat turns pink.

- Add the remaining ingredients.
- Cook and stir over medium heat for about 10 minutes.
- Transfer to a 9 x 13-inch pan and sprinkle with parmesan.
- Bake at 176 degrees for 20-25 minutes.

94. Spicy Pumpkin Casserole

Recipe

- 0.25 tsp salt
- 3 cloves of garlic
- 2 large eggs
- 119 g buttercream
- 425.24 g pumpkin puree
- 6 tbsp ricotta cheese
- 2 tbsp parmesan cheese
- 0.5 tsp dried rosemary
- 0.5 tsp dried sage
- 0.5 tsp dried thyme

Cooking

- Whisk salt, garlic, eggs, and cream with a whisk.
- Add the pumpkin puree, whisk and place the mixture in a baking dish (I used 7 × 11 inches).
- Put ricotta cheese on top and sprinkle with parmesan, rosemary, sage, and thyme.
- Bake at 176 ° C for 25-30 minutes. Sprinkle each serving with extra Parmesan and salt if desired.

95. Cheese bread with bacon

Ingredients

- 200 g bacon
- 1/2 cup almond flour
- 1 tbsp baking powder
- 1/3 cup sour cream
- large eggs
- tbsp melted butter
- 1 cup grated cheddar cheese

Cooking

- Preheat the oven to 148 degrees. Oil the baking tray. Then cut the bacon into cubes and fry it in a pan until crisp.
- Beat almond flour and baking powder.
- Beat sour cream and eggs.
- Mix wet and dry ingredients together.
- Add the butter and mix, then add the bacon and cheddar cheese.
- Put the dough in a bread pan. Garnish the top with a little cheese.
- Bake for 45 minutes, then insert a wooden toothpick into the center. The bread will be ready when the toothpick comes out clean.

- Let the bread cool before slicing, because if you cut it hot, it may fall apart. Better yet, if you keep the bread in the refrigerator before serving.

96. Chicken casserole with olives and feta cheese

Recipe

Chicken Casserole:

- 0.5 kg boneless chicken thighs
- Salt and pepper to taste
- 2 tbsp butter
- 85 g pesto
- 1¼ cup oily whipped cream
- 85 g green olives
- 140 g diced feta cheese
- clove garlic, finely chopped

To submit:

- 140 g of leafy greens
- 4 tbsp olive oil
- Salt and pepper to taste

Cooking

- Preheat the oven to 204 degrees. Cut the chicken into small pieces. Season with salt and pepper.

- Place the butter in a large pan. Heat the pan until the butter is hot, then fry the chicken pieces until they are golden brown. You may need to cook chicken in batches.
- Combine the pesto and buttercream for the sauce.
- Put chicken, olives, feta cheese, garlic and pesto in a baking dish. Mix well and bake for 30 minutes or the casserole does not brown on the edges.

97. Low-Carb Meat Lasagna with Cheese

Recipe

Meat Tomato Gravy:

- 2 tbsp olive oil
- clove of garlic
- 1 medium yellow onion
- 550 g ground beef
- tbsp low carb tomato paste
- ½ tbsp dried basil
- Salt and pepper to taste
- ½ cup of water

Dough:

- large eggs
- 280 g soft cream cheese
- tsp salt
- 5 tbsp ground psyllium powder

Cheese topping:

- 140 g grated, partially skimmed mozzarella cheese
- 400 g sour cream
- Salt and pepper to taste
- 56 g grated Parmesan cheese

- ½ cup chopped fresh parsley

Cooking

- Heat the pan over medium heat, then add the olive oil. Finely chop the garlic and onions, and sauté until tender.
- Add ground beef to the pan and sauté until brown. Mix with tomato paste, basil, salt, and pepper.
- Add water and bring to a boil. Reduce heat and simmer until water evaporates. The meat mixture should be sufficiently dry.
- Preheat the oven to 148 degrees. In a medium bowl, combine eggs, cream cheese, and salt. Continue whipping, gradually adding some psyllium powder. Leave the mixture for a few minutes.
- Place a baking sheet on parchment paper, then flatten the dough on a sheet with a spatula. Put the second piece of parchment on top and roll it out with a rolling pin.
- Leave both sheets of parchment paper in place and bake for 10-15 minutes. Remove the sheet from the oven and cool for several minutes. Remove the parchment and cut the dough into lasagna sheets.
- Increase the temperature in the oven to 204 degrees. Combine mozzarella, sour cream, salt, pepper, parsley and most of the Parmesan cheese. Leave some cheese for topping.

- Lubricate the lasagna pan, then put the dough sheet, minced meat and dough again.
- Lay the cheese mixture on top and sprinkle with the remaining parmesan.
- Bake with lasagna for about 30 minutes, or until the cheese is browned and begins to bubble.

98. Stuffed Pepper Keto Casserole

Recipe

- tbsp olive oil
- 450 g minced pork
- 450 g ground beef
- medium chopped green bell peppers
- 1/2 cup chopped onion
- cloves of garlic
- 1/2 tsp paprika
- 1 tsp Italian seasoning
- 1/2 tsp salt
- 1/4 tsp pepper
- 400 g cauliflower
- 800 g chopped sun-dried tomatoes
- 226 g chopped mozzarella

Cooking

- Preheat the oven to 176 ° C.
- Heat the olive oil in a pan over medium heat. Add pork and ground beef, peppers, onions and seasonings. Cook, stirring occasionally, until the meat is lightly browned (about 5 minutes). Remove from heat.

- Mix with sun-dried tomatoes and chopped cauliflower. Spread the mixture evenly into a 9 x 13-inch mold. Spread sliced mozzarella on top.
- Bake for 25-30 minutes or until the cheese begins to brown.

99. Stuffed Pepper Keto Casserole

Recipe

- tbsp olive oil
- 450 g minced pork
- 450 g ground beef
- medium chopped green bell peppers
- 1/2 cup chopped onion
- cloves of garlic
- 1/2 tsp paprika
- 1 tsp Italian seasoning
- 1/2 tsp salt
- 1/4 tsp pepper
- 400 g cauliflower
- 800 g chopped sun-dried tomatoes
- 226 g chopped mozzarella

Cooking

- Preheat the oven to 176 ° C.
- Heat the olive oil in a pan over medium heat. Add pork and ground beef, peppers, onions, and seasonings. Cook, stirring occasionally until the meat is lightly browned (about 5 minutes). Remove from heat.

- Mix with sun-dried tomatoes and chopped cauliflower. Spread the mixture evenly into a 9 x 13-inch mold. Spread sliced mozzarella on top.
- Bake for 25-30 minutes or until the cheese begins to brown.

100. Steak with Sliced Mushrooms

Recipe

- tbsp butter
- Salt and pepper to taste
- 113 g Rib eye steak
- 113 g chopped mushrooms
- 1 large clove of garlic (minced)
- tbsp chicken stock or as needed
- 28 g cream cheese
- 1/4 tsp Worcestershire sauce
- 1/4 tsp black pepper, for the sauce
- 1 tsp fresh parsley

Cooking

- Heat the pan over medium heat, and pour half of the oil into it. Sprinkle the steak with salt and pepper, then fry in a pan and set aside.
- Add the remaining oil to the pan. Then, when the oil becomes hot, add the mushrooms, and fry them until soft.
- Reduce the heat to a minimum, then add the garlic and continue cooking for about 1 minute.

- Pour in the chicken stock, then use a wooden spoon to scrape off the brown pieces from the bottom of the pan.
- Add cream cheese, Worcestershire sauce, and black pepper. Stir until the cheese melts in the sauce.
- Grill the steak, then pour mushroom sauce and garnish with parsley.

101. Low Carb Garlic Mushrooms

Recipe

- tbsp olive oil
- 4 garlic cloves, finely chopped
- 1 tsp sea salt
- ¼ tsp ground pepper
- 453.59 g champignon
- tbsp butter
- tbsp chopped parsley

Cooking

- Place a large non-stick pan over high heat.
- Add oil, garlic, salt, and pepper, and fry until fragrant.
- Add the mushrooms and mix well.
- Continue stirring the mushrooms and add the butter 1 tablespoon at a time, allowing each to completely melt.
- As soon as the mushrooms begin to release liquid, reduce the heat to medium and stir occasionally until all the liquid has evaporated and the mushrooms become dark brown (this will take 10-15 minutes).
- Remove from heat and mix with parsley before serving.

102. Cheeseburger Casserole with Bacon

Recipe

- 907.18 g ground beef
- 2 large cloves of garlic (minced)
- 0.5 tsp onion powder
- 453.59 g bacon, cooked and chopped
- 8 eggs
- 170 g tomato paste
- 238 g buttercream
- 0.5 tsp salt
- 0.25 tsp ground pepper
- 340 g grated cheddar cheese

Cooking

- Sauté the ground beef with garlic and onion powder.
- Drain the excess fat, and then spread the beef over the bottom of a 9 x 13-inch pan.
- Add the bacon to the meat.
- In a medium bowl, beat the eggs, tomato paste, heavy cream, salt, and pepper.
- Add 226 g of grated cheddar cheese to the egg mixture.

- Pour the egg mixture into beef and bacon. Sprinkle the remaining cheese on top.
- Bake at 176 ° C for 30-35 minutes or until the golden top.

103. Simple low carb pizza

Recipe

Dough:

- 2 cups mozzarella
- 3 tbsp soft cream cheese
- egg
- 3/4 cup almond flour
- tsp psyllium powder
- 1 tbsp Italian seasoning
- 1/2 tsp salt

Sauce:

- 1/3 cup salt-free tomato sauce
- 1/16 tsp salt
- 1/8 tsp chopped red pepper
- 1/4 tsp Italian seasoning
- 1/8 tsp black pepper

Filling:

- 12 slices of pepperoni
- 3/4 cup mozzarella

Cooking

- Preheat the oven to 204 degrees and place a baking sheet on parchment paper.
- In a microwave bowl, melt the mozzarella by stirring the cheese after 30 seconds so that it does not burn.
- In a bowl of melted mozzarella, add all the ingredients for the dough, and then mix thoroughly.
- Roll the dough into a ball and place it on 0.5-0.6 cm in a circle on a prepared baking sheet.
- Bake for 10 minutes, then remove from oven, turn over and bake for another 2 minutes.
- While preparing the dough, in a small bowl, mix the tomato sauce with salt, red pepper, Italian seasoning, and black pepper.
- Remove the crust from the oven and lay the sauce, cheese, and pepperoni on top.
- Return the pizza to the oven and bake for 5-7 minutes.
- Remove from oven; allow to cool for 5-10 minutes, chop and serve.

104. Braised Beef with Noodles and Mushrooms

Recipe

- tbsp olive oil
- 1 small onion, thinly sliced
- 1 tbsp fresh grated ginger
- garlic cloves, finely chopped
- 1 tsp chili pasta
- 1 tbsp fish sauce
- ¼ cup of soy sauce
- ¼ cup rice wine vinegar
- 113 g thinly sliced mushrooms
- Salt and pepper to taste
- 5 cups beef broth
- packs of shirataki noodles
- 10 slices of roast beef

Toppings (optional):

- Hard-boiled eggs
- Coriander
- Sesame seeds
- Chopped green onions
- Chopped seaweed

Cooking

- Heat the olive oil in a large skillet over medium heat. Sauté the onion until it is soft.
- Add ginger, garlic, chili paste, fish and soy sauce, rice wine vinegar, mushrooms, salt, pepper and beef broth.
- Cook over low heat for 30 minutes.
- Remove the noodles from the packaging and rinse with cold water. Add to the pan, and salt / pepper, if necessary.
- Serve the noodles and broth. Add beef and toppings (optional).

105. Pork chops with tomatoes and mozzarella

Recipe

- 268 g boneless pork chop (2 pcs.)
- tbsp butter
- 108 g tomatoes
- 56.67 g fresh mozzarella
- 14.79 ml olive oil
- Salt and pepper to taste

Cooking

- Rub generously with pepper and salt on each side of the pork chop.
- Heat olive and butter in a large skillet over medium heat.
- Fry the pork chops for 2-3 minutes on each side.
- Transfer the meat to a baking sheet lined with parchment paper. Put 2 slices of tomato and a slice of mozzarella on top of each chop.
- Set the roasting pan to the maximum and cook the meat for about 5 minutes, or until the cheese has melted.
- Serve with low carb or salad or vegetables.

106. Low-carb beef and eggplant skewers

Recipe

- ½ large eggplant
- 453.59 g lean ground beef
- 2 beaten eggs
- 60 g finely chopped parsley leaves
- 4 minced cloves of garlic
- 54 ml of olive oil
- ½ tsp freshly ground chili peppers
- tsp salt
- ½ tsp freshly ground black pepper
- 1 tsp oregano
- ½ tsp dried thyme
- tbsp grill oils
- Wooden skewers soaked in water

Cooking

- Cut the eggplant into circles about 1.2 cm thick.
- Sprinkle liberally with salt and set aside for 10 minutes to remove bitterness.
- In a large bowl, mix the minced meat with parsley, onion, garlic, olive oil, chili pepper, salt, black pepper, oregano,

thyme and eggs. Mix thoroughly with your hands and form the patties so that they fit into the slices of the eggplant.
- Heat a large non-stick grill pan over medium heat and lightly oil.
- Rinse the eggplant slices and gently push with your hands to squeeze out excess water.
- String the eggplant slices and meatballs on the soaked skewers, and place in a preheated grill pan.
- Cook for 15 minutes, carefully turning over several times.

107. Avocado Low Carb Burger

Recipe

- avocado
- 1 leaf lettuce
- slices of prosciutto or any ham
- 1 slice of tomato
- 1 egg
- ½ tbsp olive oil for frying

For the sauce:

- tbsp low carb mayonnaise
- ¼ tsp low carb hot sauce
- ¼ tsp mustard
- ¼ tsp Italian seasoning
- ½ tsp sesame seeds (optional)

Cooking

- In a small bowl, combine keto-friendly mayonnaise, mustard, hot sauce, and Italian seasoning.
- Heat 1/2 tablespoon of olive oil in a pan and cook an egg. The yolk must be fluid.
- Cut the avocado in half, remove the peel and bone. Cut the narrowest part of the avocado so that the fruit can stand on a plate.

- Fill the hole in one half of the avocado with the prepared sauce.
- Top with lettuce, prosciutto strips, a slice of tomato and a fried egg.
- Cover with the other half of the avocado and sprinkle with sesame seeds (optional).

108. Thai style pork roast with basil

Recipe

- 283.5 g minced pork
- ½ finely chopped chili
- 2 minced garlic cloves
- 8 g basil leaves
- ½ tbsp coconut amino acids
- ½ tsp erythritis (optional)
- 1 ½ tbsp coconut oil
- lime wedges (for serving)
- 1 tsp olive oil
- Black pepper to taste
- eggs (for serving)

Cooking

- In a small bowl, mix coconut amino acids with erythritol. Set aside.
- Heat coconut oil in a pan, add chopped garlic and chopped chili, and fry for 1 minute.
- Add minced pork and sauté for 5 minutes or until brown.
- Pour in a mixture of coconut amino acids and cook for another 1 minute, stirring constantly.

- Add basil leaves, mix and turn off the heat.
- Heat the olive oil in a pan and fry the eggs, one at a time.
- Serve with lime wedges and fried eggs seasoned with black pepper or cauliflower rice (optional).

109. Chicken thighs in creamy tomato sauce

Recipe

Chicken thighs:

- ½ cup grated parmesan
- 6 chicken thighs, skinless and boneless
- Salt and pepper to taste

Creamy Sauce:

- ¼ cup of dried tomato oil
- cup chopped sun-dried tomatoes
- 4 minced garlic cloves
- 1 tbsp Italian seasoning
- 1 ½ cup oily whipped cream
- ¼ cup parmesan cheese

Cooking

- Put on a plate of chicken parmesan, salt, and a little pepper, and mix. Coat the chicken thighs well with the mixture.
- Heat oil from sun-dried tomatoes in a large frying pan over medium heat. Fry the chicken and cheese for a few minutes on each side to brown the meat. Set aside.

- Put the sun-dried tomatoes, garlic and Italian seasoning in the pan. Cook for a few minutes until the tomatoes begin to soften.
- Add the heavy cream and sprinkle with the remaining Parmesan cheese. Whip it all together.
- Put the chicken back in the pan and simmer until cooked.

110. Baked pork chops with a cheese crust

Recipe

- 4 pork chops
- 1/2 cup grated parmesan
- 1/2 tsp garlic powder
- 1 tbsp dried parsley
- 1 tsp dried thyme
- 1 tsp paprika
- 3/4 tsp salt
- 1/2 tsp pepper
- 1/2 teaspoon onion powder
- 1/4 tsp chili powder
- 1/8 tsp oregano
- 1 tbsp avocado oil

Cooking

- Preheat the oven to 176 degrees. Grease a large baking dish with non-stick spray or oil.
- Combine the parmesan cheese and spices in a shallow dish. Beat together until smooth.
- Heat the avocado oil over medium heat in a large skillet.

- Cover the pork chops with seasoning and place on a hot frying pan (a cast-iron frying pan is perfect for a crispy crust). Fry both sides of the chops, and transfer them to the prepared baking dish. Pour the chops with a low-carb sauce.
- Bake the meat for about 50 minutes, until the internal temperature reaches 65 degrees. Remove from the oven and let cool for about 10 minutes.

111. Low carb beef roll

Recipe

- 900 g ground beef
- 1/2 tsp fine Himalayan salt
- tsp black pepper
- 1/4 cup yeast
- large eggs
- tbsp avocado oil
- 1 tbsp lemon zest
- 1/4 cup chopped parsley
- 1/4 cup chopped fresh oregano
- cloves of garlic

Cooking

- Preheat the oven to 204 degrees.
- In a large bowl, combine ground beef, salt, black pepper, and nutritional yeast.
- In a blender or food processor, beat eggs, butter, herbs, and garlic. Beat until eggs begin to froth, and then add chopped herbs, lemon zest, and garlic.
- Add the egg mixture to the minced meat and mix.

- Pour the meat mixture into a small 8 x 4-inch dish. Smooth well.
- Put on the middle rack and bake for 50-60 minutes, until the top turns golden brown.
- Carefully remove from the oven and tilt the mold over the sink to drain all the liquid. Allow cooling for 5-10 minutes before slicing.
- Garnish with fresh lemon and serve.

112. Crispy Ginger Mackerel with Vegetables

Recipe

Marinade:

- tbsp grated ginger
- 1 tbsp lemon juice
- tbsp olive oil
- 1 tbsp coconut amino acids
- Salt and pepper to taste

Fish:

- 2 (about 226 g) boneless mackerel filet
- 28 g almonds
- ½ cup broccoli
- tbsp oils
- ½ small yellow onion
- 1/3 cup diced red bell pepper
- small sun-dried tomatoes (chopped)
- tbsp mashed avocado

Cooking

- Preheat the oven to 204 ° C. Place a baking sheet on parchment paper or foil.

- Combine grated ginger, lemon juice, olive oil, coconut amino acids, and a little salt and pepper. Grate the mackerel fillet with half the marinade.
- Place the fillet on a baking sheet with the skin up. Bake for 12-15 minutes or until the skin becomes crisp.
- Place the almonds on a separate baking sheet. Cook for 5-6 minutes or until the nuts turn brown. Remove from the oven and cool before chopping.
- Lightly steam the broccoli until it begins to soften, but becomes soft. Cut into pieces.
- Heat the pan over medium heat, then add the oil and let it melt. Sauté the onions and peppers until they are soft.
- Add broccoli and sun-dried tomatoes, and continue cooking until they heat up.
- Turn off the heat, then mix with the rest of the dressing and roasted almonds. Serve with the avocado smoothie.

113. Spinach Egg Casserole

Recipe

- 283.5 g spinach
- ¼ chopped onion
- minced garlic
- 56.7 g cream cheese
- 59.5 ml buttercream
- 1 tbsp butter
- 1/8 tsp ground nutmeg
- eggs
- Salt and pepper to taste
- 1 tbsp grated Parmesan cheese

Cooking

- Boil water in a pan, add salt and spinach and simmer for 1 minute. Drain the spinach, squeeze, chop and set aside.
- Heat the oil in a pan, add chopped onion and garlic, and cook for 3 minutes or until it becomes aromatic. Add cream cheese and heavy cream, and cook until smooth.
- Add chopped spinach and cook for 10 minutes. Season with nutmeg, salt, and pepper.
- Preheat the oven to 204 degrees.

- Put the spinach in a baking dish and make small indentations with the back of the spoon.
- Break into each hole in the egg.
- Bake for up to 15 minutes or until egg whites is cooked.
- Season the casserole with salt and pepper. Serve sprinkled with grated Parmesan cheese.

114. Thai fried chicken with cashew nuts

Recipe

- 283.5 g diced chicken
- 1/4 onion, sliced
- ½ sweet pepper, sliced
- 32.25 g cashew
- clove garlic
- ½ tsp chopped chili peppers
- 1 tsp hot low carb sauce
- 1 ½ tbsp coconut amino acids
- ½ tsp grated fresh ginger
- tbsp coconut oil
- 1 tbsp chopped green onions
- 1 tsp black sesame seeds

Cooking

- Heat the pan and saute the cashews until brown. Set aside.
- Add coconut oil to the pan and heat to medium temperature. Add the diced chicken and cook for 5 minutes or until tender.
- When the chicken is cooked, add onion, bell pepper, chopped garlic, ginger, and hot sauce to the pan. Mix well, add chopped chili and cook over high heat for 3 minutes.

- Add coconut amino acids, cashews and cook for another 2 minutes to evaporate the liquid. Turn off the heat, add chopped green onions and mix well.
- Transfer to a bowl and serve, sprinkling with sesame seeds.

115. Low carb steaks with cauliflower puree

Recipe

- 3 cups of cauliflower flowers
- tbsp butter
- tbsp unsweetened almond milk
- 340 g ground beef
- ¼ cup almond flour
- tsp fresh chopped parsley
- 2 tsp Worcestershire sauce
- ¼ tsp onion powder
- ¼ tsp garlic powder
- Salt and pepper to taste
- 1 tbsp olive oil
- 1 ½ cup chopped mushrooms
- ¼ beef broth
- 2 tbsp sour cream

Cooking

- Boil a pot of water and season with plenty of salt. Add the cauliflower and cook for 10 minutes or until tender.
- Drain the cauliflower, and then transfer it to a bowl to crush with butter and almond milk. Set aside.

- Preheat the oven to 190 degrees. Line the baking sheet with foil.
- In a bowl, combine ground beef, almond flour, parsley, Worcestershire sauce, onion and garlic powder, salt, and pepper.
- Divide the mixture into steak patties, and then place them on a baking sheet with foil. Bake for 20 minutes or until tender.
- Heat a large frying pan over medium heat with olive oil to make the mushroom sauce. Add mushrooms and fry until they are soft and brown.
- Pour in beef broth and stir often, scraping pieces from the bottom of the pan.
- Add sour cream and mix, and then remove the pan from the heat. Season with salt and pepper to taste.
- Serve steaks with mashed cauliflower by pouring mushroom sauce on top.

116. Almond Noodles (Pasta)

Recipe

- cup almond flour
- tbsp sifted coconut flour
- tsp xanthan gum
- 1/4 tsp sea salt
- 2 tsp raw apple cider vinegar
- large egg, slightly beaten
- 2-4 tsp Water as needed

To submit:

- ¼ cup butter
- 2 cloves of minced garlic
- 2 tbsp olive oil
- 2 tbsp grated cheese (cheddar, mozzarella or to your taste)

Cooking

- Combine almond and coconut flour, xanthan gum and salt in a medium-sized bowl.
- Add vinegar and egg. Mix well until smooth, gradually adding water.

- Form a ball from the dough, wrap it in plastic wrap and refrigerate for 30 minutes.
- Now roll out the dough as thinly as possible.
- Cut the pasta into strips about 2.5 cm wide. Then cut the strips into small rectangles using a pasta knife or a regular knife. Squeeze the rectangles in the middle to turn them into a butterfly.
- Put the pasta in the freezer for 10-15 minutes.
- Fry the butter in a pan over medium heat and add olive oil.
- Add garlic and fry until fragrant.
- Put the pasta in the pan and cook until al dente - about 3-4 minutes. Since these are fresh pasta, do not digest them.
- Add the fried garlic, sprinkle with cheese and serve.

117. Chicken Breasts with White Sauce

Recipe

- 4 medium-sized chicken breasts
- 240 g coconut cream
- 240 g of white wine
- 300 g of mushrooms
- 300 g green beans (halves)
- 2 tsp Dijon mustard
- 4 cloves of garlic
- 54 g of olive oil
- tsp fresh chopped thyme
- 1 tsp salt
- 1 tsp pepper

Cooking

- Preheat the oven to 180 degrees.
- Heat the pan to medium temperature with half the amount of olive oil needed for the recipe. Sauté chicken breasts for 2 minutes on each side.
- Place the chicken on a baking sheet lined with baking paper. Cook for 15 minutes.
- Meanwhile, in the same pan, chop the mushrooms and lightly fry them using the remaining olive oil and garlic.

- Add beans, coconut cream, white wine, Dijon mustard, thyme, salt, and pepper. Stir in a pan, reduce heat and bring to a boil.
- Serve the breasts in the sauce, with mushrooms and beans.

118. Creamy Pumpkin Muffins

Recipe

Cream Cheese Filling:

- 170 g soft cream cheese
- 3 tbsp erythritol powder
- tbsp greasy whipped cream
- ½ tsp vanilla

Muffins:

- 2 cup almond flour
- ½ cup erythritis
- ¼ cup non-flavored protein powder
- 2 tsp baking powder
- 2 tsp pumpkin spices
- ½ tsp salt
- 2 large eggs
- ½ cup pumpkin puree
- ¼ cup melted butter
- ¼ cup unsweetened almond milk
- ½ tsp vanilla extract

Cooking

- Mix all the ingredients of the creamy filling until a uniform dough is formed.
- Preheat the oven to 162 degrees and layout the muffin mold with paper inserts. You can also use silicone.
- In a medium bowl, combine almond flour, sweetener, protein powder, baking powder, pumpkin spices, and salt.
- Mix eggs, pumpkin puree, ghee, almond milk, and vanilla extract.
- Add a spoonful of batter to each pan, then make a notch in the dough for the filling. Add the filling with a spoon, then cover it with a little dough.
- Bake for 25 minutes.

119. Shirataki noodles with cheese

Recipe

- 600 g shirataki noodles
- 169.5 g grated cheddar cheese
- 120 g coconut milk
- 59.5 g full of whipped cream
- large egg
- 1 tsp Dijon mustard
- 0.13 tsp garlic powder
- 7 g chopped greaves

Cooking

- Drain and rinse the shirataki noodles well. Put in boiling water for 3 minutes, then strain if necessary.
- Transfer the noodles to a clean towel and wring out to absorb excess moisture. If necessary, cut the noodles into shorter pieces.
- Put the noodles on a dry frying pan over low heat and stir for 5-10 minutes to make it as dry as possible.
- Mix the noodles, cheese, coconut milk, cream, egg, mustard, and garlic powder.

- Transfer the mixture to a baking dish of 8 × 8 inches, sprinkle with chopped cracklings on top.
- Bake at a temperature of 176 degrees for 20-25 minutes.]

120. Crispy squash pie

Recipe

- 6 large eggs
- 500 g chopped zucchini
- 84 g almond flour
- 30 g coconut flour
- 113 g grated cheddar cheese
- 109 g coconut oil
- 2 tbsp fresh parsley (chopped)
- 2 tbsp grated parmesan cheese
- tbsp chopped dry onions
- minced garlic cloves
- 0.5 tsp dried basil
- 0.5 tsp salt

Cooking

- Preheat the oven to 176 ° C and oil a 9.5-inch mold.
- Combine all the ingredients in a large bowl, then transfer to the prepared form.
- Bake for 45-60 minutes or until cooked.
- Remove from the oven and cool on a stand.

121. Low-Carbon Baked Beans with Beef

Recipe

- 3 slices of bacon
- 455 g lean ground beef
- tbsp dried chopped onions
- 0.25 tsp garlic powder
- 430 g canned beans/beans
- 62.5 g of water
- 450 g canned tomato paste
- 59.75 g apple cider vinegar
- 20 drops of stevia
- tsp liquid smoke
- 1 tsp salt
- 0.25 tsp ground black pepper

Cooking

- Sauté the bacon over medium heat until brown. Crumble and set aside.
- In the same pan, sauté the ground beef with dried onions and garlic powder until the beef is evenly brown.
- Return the bacon to the pan. Add drained beans/beans, water, tomato paste, stevia, vinegar, and liquid smoke. Season with salt and pepper.
- Put on a baking sheet, cover and bake at 176 degrees for 1 hour.

122. Simple stew with beef stew

Recipe

- 910 g diced beef
- 3 tbsp olive oil
- 910 g beef broth
- liter of water
- 1 tsp seasonings such as thyme, rosemary and / or oregano
- 1 tsp parsley
- 1 tsp chopped garlic
- tsp salt
- 0.5 tsp ground black pepper
- 230 g of radish (or turnip), diced
- 1 small carrot chopped into small pieces
- celery stalks, sliced in half
- 1 tsp xanthan gum

Cooking

- Sauté the beef in olive oil. Add beef broth, water, and seasonings. Bring to a boil, then reduce heat, cover and simmer for 1 hour.
- Add vegetables, sprinkle with xanthan gum, cover and simmer for another 1 hour.

123. Creamy Cheese Soup with Broccoli

Recipe

- 2 cloves of chopped garlic
- 2 tbsp butter
- 238 g buttercream
- 250 g unsweetened almond milk
- 1.44kg of chicken stock
- 0.5 tsp salt
- 3 tbsp Dijon mustard
- 0.5 tsp cayenne pepper
- tsp dried tarragon leaves
- 283 g minced broccoli
- 283 g grated cauliflower
- 339 g grated cheddar cheese

Cooking

- Sauté the garlic in melted butter in a large saucepan over medium heat until golden brown.
- Add cream, milk, chicken stock, salt, mustard, cayenne pepper, and tarragon. Bring to a boil.
- Add chopped broccoli and cauliflower. Bring to a boil.
- Reduce heat to a minimum and cook for about 5-10 minutes, stirring occasionally.
- Add the cheese and simmer until the cheese melts.

124. Green Bean Chicken Casserole

Recipe

- 306 g green beans
- chicken cooked and minced
- 450 g cream cheese
- 238 g butter whipped cream
- 250 g of water
- 1 tsp garlic powder
- 0.5 tsp salt
- 50 g grated Parmesan cheese
- 56 g grated mozzarella

Cooking

- Make green beans, then place them in a lightly oiled 9 × 13-inch baking dish.
- Heat cream, water, cream cheese, garlic powder, salt and Parmesan cheese over low heat, stirring until smooth.
- Pour the beans with 1 cup of sauce.
- Top the chicken and pour the rest of the sauce.
- Top with mozzarella and parmesan cheese.
- Bake at 176 degrees for about 25 minutes or until the cheese is browned.

125. Asparagus Stuffed Chicken Breasts

Recipe

- 900 g skinless bones of chicken breasts (4 breasts)
- 2 tsp fresh thyme
- 54 g of olive oil
- 2 tbsp balsamic vinegar or red wine
- 3 cloves of garlic
- 0.25 tsp salt
- 12 asparagus pods

Cooking

- Preheat the oven to 190 ° C.
- In a small bowl, combine olive oil, vinegar, garlic, and salt. Set aside.
- Hammer each chicken breast to a thickness of about 0.5 cm.
- Season the chicken breasts with salt and pepper to taste.
- Place 3 asparagus pods in the middle of each flattened chicken breast. Wrap chicken around asparagus and secure with toothpicks. Put the stuffed chicken in a baking dish, then evenly pour olive oil.
- Bake for 25-30 minutes until the chicken is fully cooked. Remove the toothpicks before serving.

125. Stuffed Tomatoes with Minced Meat and Cheese

Recipe

- 10 medium tomatoes
- 4550 g ground beef
- 56.5 g cheddar cheese or mozzarella
- 10 slices of thin cheddar cheese
- 3 tbsp olive oil for lubrication
- Parsley for decoration

Cooking

- Preheat the oven to 176 ° C.
- Fry the ground beef in a lightly greased pan for several minutes.
- Wash the tomatoes thoroughly with cold water. Wipe with a clean cloth.
- Cut a thin slice at the end of the tomato so that each tomato stands correctly. Cut off the top of the tomato to make a hole.
- Spoon the inside of each tomato.
- Lightly grease the outside of the tomatoes with olive oil.
- Put thin slices of cheese around the tomatoes and fill each with minced meat. Sprinkle with grated cheese.

- Bake for 5-8 minutes or until the cheese melts and turns golden. Feel free to add more cheese if you want the cheese to overflow or drip on the sides.
- Allow to cool for 1-2 minutes and slowly shift to a dish.
- Garnish with fresh chopped parsley.

126. Crispy Bacon Chicken Pizza

Recipe

Crust:

- 40 g chopped mozzarella
- 30 g grated Parmesan cheese
- tsp Italian seasoning: basil, oregano, rosemary and thyme
- 1 large egg
- Salt and ground black pepper to taste (I used 1/4 salt and pepper)

Sauce:

- 1/3 cup keto mayonnaise
- 1/3 cup sour cream
- 1/4 tsp dried green onions
- 1/4 tsp dried parsley
- 1/4 tsp dried dill
- 1/4 tsp garlic powder
- 1/8 tsp onion powder
- 1/8 tsp salt
- Pinch of pepper

Filling:

- 100 g chopped mozzarella

- 85 g diced tomatoes
- 3 slices of bacon, cooked and chopped

Cooking

- Preheat the oven to 204 ° C. Place the pizza baking sheet on parchment paper.
- Combine the crust ingredients in a large bowl, then roll the ball.
- Place the meatball on parchment paper. Cover with a second sheet of parchment paper and roll into a large circle. Remove the top parchment paper.
- Bake the crust for 20-25 minutes or until it is browned.
- While the base is baking, mix the ingredients for the sauce.
- Remove the crust from the oven, turn it over and remove the parchment.
- Crust about 1/2 cup of sauce, then sprinkle 1/2 cup of mozzarella cheese. Sprinkle with bacon and diced tomatoes. Sprinkle the remaining half of mozzarella cheese on top.
- Return the pizza to the oven and bake for about 10 minutes. Cut into 8 slices and serve with the remaining sauce.

127. Low Carb Chicken Noodle Soup

Recipe

- 3 tbsp coconut oil
- 3 minced cloves of garlic
- chopped onion
- 0.5 tsp ground turmeric
- 1 medium turnip, diced
- 8 stalks of celery, chopped
- l chicken bone broth
- 450 g pre-cooked and chopped chicken
- 4 tsp fresh chopped basil
- 4 tsp fresh chopped parsley
- 0.5 tsp sea salt
- bay leaves
- 455 g zucchini chopped with spirals

Cooking

- Heat 1 tablespoon of coconut oil in a saucepan over medium heat. Add garlic and fry until fragrant.
- Add onions and turmeric. Cook until onion is clear.
- Add turnips and celery with the remaining 2 tablespoons of coconut oil. Cook for about 10 minutes.

- Add the broth, chicken, basil, parsley, salt and bay leaf. Bring to a boil, then reduce heat.
- Cover and simmer for about 40 minutes. Remove from heat.
- Remove the bay leaf. Add the spiralized zucchini and cover the pan. Leave to brew for 10 minutes to soften the zucchini noodles.

128. Low Carb Chicken Noodle Soup

Recipe

- 3 tbsp coconut oil
- 3 minced cloves of garlic
- chopped onion
- 0.5 tsp ground turmeric
- 1 medium turnip, diced
- 8 stalks of celery, chopped
- l chicken bone broth
- 450 g pre-cooked and chopped chicken
- 4 tsp fresh chopped basil
- 4 tsp fresh chopped parsley
- 0.5 tsp sea salt
- bay leaves
- 455 g zucchini chopped with spirals

Cooking

- Heat 1 tablespoon of coconut oil in a saucepan over medium heat. Add garlic and fry until fragrant.
- Add onions and turmeric. Cook until onion is clear.
- Add turnips and celery with the remaining 2 tablespoons of coconut oil. Cook for about 10 minutes.

- Add the broth, chicken, basil, parsley, salt and bay leaf. Bring to a boil, then reduce heat.
- Cover and simmer for about 40 minutes. Remove from heat.
- Remove the bay leaf. Add the spiralized zucchini and cover the pan. Leave to brew for 10 minutes to soften the zucchini noodles.

129. Creamy Salmon Soup with Coconut Milk
Recipe

- 908 g chicken bone broth
- 2 tbsp lard or coconut oil
- 1 small chopped onion
- 4 minced cloves of garlic
- 2 medium turnips, peeled and diced
- 2 medium carrots, chopped
- 3 stalks of celery, chopped
- 1 tbsp cider vinegar
- 5 sprigs of fresh thyme, chopped
- 0.5 tsp sea salt (or more to taste)
- 455 g sliced salmon fillet
- 400 g canned coconut milk
- 2 tbsp lime juice or lemon juice
- 2 green chopped onions (optional)

Cooking

- Melt lard or coconut oil in a large saucepan. Sauté the onion until transparent (about 5 minutes).
- Add the garlic and continue to simmer until fragrant. Then add turnips, carrots, and celery. Cook for another 5-10 minutes until the vegetables are lightly browned.
- Add the broth, vinegar, thyme, and salt. Reduce heat, cover and simmer for 30 minutes to soften vegetables.

- Put 2 cups of soup in a blender (remove the carrots so that the liquid does not turn orange) and beat everything until smooth. Add mashed potatoes to the remaining soup.
- Add salmon and coconut milk, and continue cooking until the fish is cooked.
- Season with lime (or lemon) juice and garnish with green onions.

130. Cabbage Puree with Bacon

Recipe

- 455 g brussels sprouts
- 1 tbsp olive oil
- 6 strips of bacon
- 80 g chopped onion
- 940 g chicken bone broth
- 0.5 tsp sea salt

Cooking

- Fill the baking sheet with foil. Cut the brussels sprouts in half. Put the cabbage with the cut side down on the foil and drizzle with olive oil. Bake at 218 degrees for 25 minutes, turning each half in about 12 minutes.
- While the cabbage is baking, fry the bacon in a large pan or roasting pan. When the bacon is ready, put it on paper towels.
- In the fat remaining in the pan, cook the onion until transparent. Add the broth and salt. Bring to a boil and cook for 5-10 minutes.
- Cut the bacon and add to the half of the soup along with fried Brussels sprouts. Let it brew for another 5 minutes.
- Mix the soup until smooth with a blender. Serve with chopped pieces of bacon.

131. Low carb egg noodles

Recipe

- 3 egg yolks
- 113.4 g soft cream cheese
- 0.13 tsp garlic powder
- 33.33 g fresh grated Parmesan cheese (about 1/3 cup plus 2 tablespoons)
- 37.33 g of freshly grated mozzarella cheese (about 1/3 cup plus 2 tablespoons)
- 0.13 tsp dried basil
- 0.13 tsp dried marjoram
- 0.13 tsp dried tarragon
- 0.13 tsp ground oregano
- 0.13 tsp ground black pepper

Cooking

- Beat egg yolks and cream cheese together. Add the parmesan and mozzarella, and continue whisking. Sprinkle with spices and beat well again.
- Put a baking sheet on parchment, and evenly distribute the cheese-egg mixture on it. Smooth with a spatula or the back of a spoon.

- Place the pan in the preheated oven to 246 ° C and reduce the temperature to 176 ° C.
- Bake 5 to 8 minutes. If small bubbles begin to appear, reduce the temperature to 148 ° C and continue to bake for 2-3 minutes until cooked.
- Let cool at room temperature for 10 to 15 minutes. Slice with a regular pizza knife or knife.

132. Cheeseburger Low-Carb Pie

Recipe

- 450 g ground beef
- 160 g chopped onion
- 0.5 tsp salt
- 40 g coconut flour
- 3 tbsp almond flour
- 1 tsp baking powder
- 250 g unsweetened almond milk
- 4 large eggs
- 170 g grated cheese
- 1 tomato (optional)

Cooking

- Fry the ground beef and onions in a pan until the meat turn brown, about 8-10 minutes.
- Place the beef mixture in a bowl and sprinkle with salt.
- Combine coconut and almond flour, baking powder, almond milk, and eggs.
- Pour the egg mixture evenly over the meat. Sprinkle 1 cup of cheese on top.
- Bake at 204 ° C for about 25 minutes.

- Remove from the oven and add the tomato and remaining cheese if desired.
- Bake another 5 minutes.

133. Mushroom roll with nuts and spinach

Recipe

Roll

- 227 g of any kind of mushrooms
- 2 tbsp chopped thyme
- 5 eggs (protein separated from the yolks)
- 15 g unsalted butter
- 2 cloves of chopped garlic
- 1/2 tsp salt
- 1/2 tsp black pepper

Filling

- 180 g spinach
- 56 g soft cream cheese
- 50 g chopped walnuts
- 25 g grated Parmesan cheese

Cooking

- Preheat the oven to 200 degrees.
- Heat the butter in a frying pan over medium heat.
- Add the garlic and fry for 2-3 minutes.
- Finely chop the mushrooms and add to the pan.

- Fry for 8-10 minutes until mushrooms are ready.
- Add thyme, and season with salt and pepper. Remove from heat.
- Put the mushroom mixture in a bowl, add the egg yolks and beat well (I use a hand blender) until smooth.
- In another bowl, beat the egg whites.
- Gently pour the egg whites into the mushroom mixture.
- Lubricate with butter and place a rectangular baking sheet on parchment.
- Spread the dough evenly in a baking sheet and bake for 15 minutes until it is firm and slightly golden.
- While preparing the roll, prepare the filling: mix cream cheese, spinach and parmesan well.
- When the roll is ready, remove it from the oven and carefully cut the edges with a knife.
- Place the roll on a large piece of parchment paper and tap on the baking sheet so that the roll comes out.
- Remove the parchment that was used for baking the roll from its top.
- Spread the cheese and spinach on a roll and sprinkle with chopped walnuts.
- Using parchment paper underneath, roll up the roll.
- Remove the parchment and serve.

134. Meat muffins

Recipe

- 226 g ground beef
- 226 g of minced chicken
- ¼ cup grated cheddar cheese
- 1 egg (slightly beaten)
- 1 tsp hot low carb sauce
- 1 tbsp fresh chopped parsley (plus a side dish)
- ½ tsp garlic powder
- 1/4 tsp sea salt
- 1/8 tsp black pepper
- 1 tsp olive oil for lubrication
- Topping
- ¼ cup low carb sauce
- 1 tsp mustard

Cooking

- Preheat the oven to 190 degrees.
- Combine all ingredients (except olive oil and topping ingredients) in a large bowl. Beat well.
- Pour the dough into muffin tins and bake for 10-15 minutes.
- While the muffins are baking, topping. Just beat the mustard and ketchup in a bowl.

- Remove the muffins from the oven and pour them over the cooked sauce. You can also sprinkle them with grated cheese.
- Put in the oven and bake another 8-10 minutes.
- Remove from the oven and let cool for 5-10 minutes. Garnish with fresh parsley.

135. Jalapeno cheese biscuits

Recipe

- 56 g coconut flour
- 84 g unsalted butter (soft)
- 2-3 jalapenos peppers (chopped)
- 1 egg
- 170 g grated cheddar cheese

Cooking

- Put all the ingredients in a food processor and beat until smooth.
- Put the mass on a sheet of parchment paper and give it the shape of a roll. Fold it with parchment paper.
- Refrigerate for at least 30 minutes.
- Preheat the oven to 180 degrees.
- Unfold the parchment paper and cut the roll into pieces. Put slices on a baking sheet with parchment and bake for 20-25 minutes, until they become hard and golden.

136. Jalapeno Low Carb Bagels

Recipe

- 224 g grated mozzarella
- 56.7 g cream cheese
- 112 g almond flour
- 4.93 g of baking powder
- 3 jalapenos peppers
- 2 eggs
- 28.35 g grated cheddar cheese

Cooking

- Preheat the oven to 200 degrees.
- Chop the jalapenos. Set aside some thin circles for decoration.
- Combine almond flour and baking powder.
- Add chopped jalapenos and eggs. Mix well.
- In another bowl, combine mozzarella and cream cheese. Put the bowl in the microwave for 2 minutes, stirring after 1 minute.
- Stir well, then add the almond flour mixture.
- Stir well until a dough is formed.
- Divide the dough into 6 slices and roll them to get a bagel shape.

- Garnish the bagels with chopped jalapenos and sprinkle with grated cheddar cheese.
- Bake for 20-30 minutes until golden brown.

137. Cheeseburger Low Carb Casserole

Recipe

- 1 tbsp chopped garlic
- 1 kg lean ground beef
- 85 g diced cream cheese
- ½ tsp salt
- 1 tsp onion powder
- ¼ tsp pepper
- 4 eggs
- ½ cup oily whipped cream
- 1 ½ cup grated cheddar cheese
- 2 tbsp regular or Dijon mustard

Cooking

- Preheat the oven to 190 ° C, then oil the baking dish.
- In a large frying pan over medium heat, fry the garlic until fragrant.
- Add ground beef and fry until cooked. Drain excess fat, then add cream cheese, salt, and pepper.
- Stir until smooth until the cream cheese melts, then transfer the mixture to the cooked form.

- Add eggs, greasy whipped cream, 1 cup grated cheddar cheese and mustard to the bowl, and beat with a blender.
- Pour the egg mixture over the ground beef, sprinkle the remaining grated cheddar cheese on top.
- Bake for about 15-18 minutes until the edges are golden brown, then turn off the oven and leave the pan inside for 2 minutes.
- Remove the casserole from the oven and let cool before serving.

138. Frittata with caramelized onions and cabbage

Recipe

- 1 large yellow onion (thinly sliced)
- 2 tbsp herbal oil
- 1 cup cabbage of your choice
- 1/4 cup water
- 3/4 tsp salt
- 1/4 tsp ground pepper
- 8 large eggs
- 1/2 cup unsweetened milk or cream

Cooking

- Heat a large frying pan over medium heat and melt the butter. Add chopped onion, 1/2 teaspoon of salt and a pinch of pepper.
- Cook the onion for 7-10 minutes until it turns golden brown. If the onion starts to burn, add a few tablespoons of water.
- Add the cabbage and simmer with the onion for 2-3 minutes until it withers. Remove the pan from the heat and let cool.
- Preheat the oven to 176 ° C and oil the baking dish.
- Add eggs, milk, 1/4 teaspoon of salt and a pinch of pepper in a blender or bowl. Stir well until light and airy.

- Put the onions and cabbage in the previously prepared form, pour the egg mixture on top.
- Bake for 25-30 minutes until the top is golden brown.
- If you want, you can sprinkle the dish with grated cheese.

139. Focaccia Low Carb Bread

Recipe

- 336 g almond flour
- g of baking powder
- 29.57 g of psyllium powder
- 2.46 g of salt
- 4.93 g oregano
- 4 egg whites
- 183 g milk or almond milk
- 62.5 g boiling water

Topping

- 54 g of olive oil
- 4.93 g of salt
- 3 sun-dried tomatoes
- 6 black olives

Cooking

- Preheat the oven to 200 degrees.
- Oil and spread a square baking dish with parchment paper.
- Mix almond flour, baking powder, psyllium powder, oregano and salt in a bowl.

- In a separate bowl, beat the egg whites until foamy.
- Add milk to the dry mix and stir to make a smooth dough.
- Add egg whites, boiling water and mix gently.
- Pour the dough into a baking dish and smooth evenly.
- Cut the dried tomatoes in strips, and cut the olives in half. Put on top of the dough.
- With a wet finger, make dimples on the test.
- Sprinkle bread with olive oil and season with salt.
- Bake for 20-25 minutes until golden brown. Allow cooling for 5 minutes.

140. Toasted Tofu with Peanut Sauce

Recipe

- 1 piece extra hard tofu
- 5 tbsp natural peanut butter
- 2 tbsp liquid amino acids
- 2 tbsp sesame oil
- 1 tbsp lime juice
- 1 tsp chili powder
- 1 tbsp a mixture of erythritol and stevia
- 1 tbsp coconut oil
- 1 small red bell pepper, diced
- 5 medium lettuce
- 1 tbsp chopped peanuts
- 2 small green onions, chopped

Cooking

- Preheat the pan on the stove. Cut the tofu into cubes about 2.5 cm in size and dry with a towel.
- Mix in a bowl natural peanut butter, liquid amino acids, sesame oil, chili powder, lime juice, and a sweetener. Mix well until smooth.

- Melt coconut oil in a pan. Sauté the tofu cubes and diced red pepper until the edges of the tofu turn a little brown.
- Add half the peanut sauce to the tofu and cook over medium heat for 1-2 minutes, stirring constantly. Once the sauce begins to thicken, remove from heat.
- Put the fried tofu and sauce on lettuce leaves.
- Pour in the remaining sauce, and garnish with chopped peanuts and green onions.

141. Delicious low-carb buns

Recipe

- 226 g cream cheese
- 3 cups grated mozzarella cheese
- 2 cup almond flour
- 4 tbsp baking powder
- 4 small eggs
- 2 tbsp unsalted butter

Cooking

- Preheat the oven to 176 ° C.
- Combine mozzarella and cream cheese in a bowl and microwave for 1 minute to completely melt the cheeses.
- Remove the bowl from the microwave and let it cool before mixing eggs, baking powder and almond flour. Mix the ingredients together and leave for 10-20 minutes.
- Oil the baking dish. Form about 15 balls from the mixture and put them into the mold.
- Put in a preheated oven for 20-30 minutes. When the buns become golden brown, fluffy and fried, remove them from the oven and serve.

142. Creamy Cheese Soup with Broccoli

Recipe

- 1 tbsp butter
- 1 chopped small onion
- 2 medium chopped garlic cloves
- Salt and pepper to taste
- ½ tsp xanthan gum
- ½ cup chicken stock
- 1 cup chopped broccoli
- 1 cup of fat cream
- 1 ½ cup grated cheddar cheese

Cooking

- Preheat the pan on the stove. Put onion, chopped garlic, salt, pepper, and oil in it, and cook over medium heat until soft.
- Add xanthan gum and chicken stock. Mix well.
- Put the broccoli in the pan and make sure it is covered with the stock.
- Quickly add cream. Bring the soup to a boil, stirring often.
- Slowly start adding cheese, stirring again.
- Serve with plenty of broccoli and cheese.

143. Homemade bread with walnuts

Recipe

- 60 g coconut flour
- 14.79 g of baking powder
- 29.57 g of psyllium powder
- 2.46 g of salt
- 4 eggs
- 59.15 g of olive or coconut oil
- 29.57 g apple cider vinegar
- 117 g chopped walnuts
- 125 g boiling water

Cooking

- Preheat the oven to 180 C.
- Combine baking powder, coconut flour, psyllium powder, and salt.
- Add eggs and butter, and mix well until the mixture looks like crackers.
- Add apple cider vinegar and mix again.
- Add chopped walnuts and mix.
- Gently add some water (you may not need this step).

- Place the baking sheet with parchment, then roll a large ball from the dough.
- Lay the dough on a baking sheet, and bake for 35-40 minutes until golden brown.

144. Homemade bread with rosemary and olives

Recipe

- 60 g coconut flour
- 4 medium eggs
- 59.15 g of olive oil
- 29.57 g of psyllium powder
- 14.79 g apple cider vinegar
- 14.79 g of baking powder
- 2.46 g of salt
- 22.18 g of rosemary (dried or fresh)
- 75 g chopped olives or olives
- 125 g boiling water

Cooking

- Heat the oven to 180 degrees.
- Put coconut flour, baking powder, rosemary, psyllium powder and salt in a bowl and mix thoroughly.
- Add the eggs and butter, then mix until the mixture looks like crackers.
- Add apple cider vinegar and mix well.
- Add chopped olives/olives and mix.
- Gently add a little water and mix again (you may not need this step).

- Put the baking sheet with parchment paper, and then roll a large ball from the dough.
- Place the dough on a baking sheet, then bake for 35 minutes until golden.

145. Low-Carbon Seed Bread

Recipe

- 33.5 g of sunflower seeds
- 16 g pumpkin seeds
- 14.79 g chia seeds
- 60 g coconut flour
- 29.57 g of flax flour
- 2 eggs
- 4 egg whites
- 29.57 g coconut oil
- 14.79 g of baking powder
- 29.57 g of psyllium powder
- 14.79 g apple cider vinegar
- 2.46 g of salt
- 125 g boiling water

Cooking

- Preheat the oven to 180 degrees.
- Lubricate and lay out the base of the bread pan with a strip of parchment paper.
- Combine coconut flour, psyllium powder, baking powder, salt, flax flour, sunflower seeds, pumpkin seeds, chia seeds in a bowl (leave a couple of tablespoons of pumpkin and sunflower seeds to sprinkle).
- Add eggs and mix thoroughly.

- Add oil and mix until smooth and slightly sticky.
- Add apple cider vinegar and stir. The dough may bubble and change color due to the chemical reaction of vinegar, do not be alarmed!
- Add a little water until you get a texture that looks like dough.
- Pour the mixture into a bread pan, smoothing it evenly.
- Sprinkle the remaining seeds on top.
- Bake for 30 to 35 minutes.

146. Fish in tomato sauce

Ingredients

- 4 frozen white fish fillets of your choice
- 2 cups cherry tomatoes cut in half
- 2 finely sliced garlic cloves
- 120 ml light chicken broth
- 60 ml of dry white wine (or use more chicken stock)
- 1/2 teaspoon salt
- 1/2 teaspoon black pepper
- 1/4 cup finely chopped fresh basil leaves (to garnish)

Preparation

- Place the tomatoes, garlic, salt, and pepper in a pan over medium heat. Cook for 5 minutes or until tomatoes are soft.
- Add chicken broth, white wine (if used), frozen fish fillets, and chopped basil. Cover and simmer 20-25 minutes, until the fish is fully cooked.
- Finally, sprinkle with an additional handful of chopped basil and serve on a bed of rice, couscous or quinoa, if desired.

147. Sea Bass and Peppers Salad

Ingredients

- Seabass was very clean: A fillet of 150 g.
- Assorted lettuces: 100 g.
- Chives: To taste
- Fresh or roasted red pepper: 1
- Cherry tomatoes To taste
- Garlic clove and parsley 1
- Leek 1
- Carrot 1
- Olive oil One tablespoon
- Salt and lemon to taste

Directions

1. We put the fillet of sea bass in aluminum foil. In the mortar, chop the garlic and parsley, add 2 small teaspoons of oil and cover the fillet of sea bass with it.
2. We also put some leek and carrot strips on the sea bass fillet (the vegetable ribbons can be made with the fruit peeler) and a little salt. Now we close the foil tightly and take it into the oven at 120 °C for 8-10 minutes. Once cooked, let it cool.
3. In a salad bowl, we put the lettuce mixture and chop the chives and pepper very finely. We add it too. Add the cherry tomatoes cut into quarters. Add only a small teaspoon of olive oil, salt,

and lemon as a dressing and stir well and now add the fish with the vegetables that we have cooked in the oven and ready to eat

148. Mexican baked beans and rice

Ingredients

- 5 ml (1 teaspoon) unsalted butter
- 1 chopped yellow onion
- 3/4 cup (190 mL) basmati rice
- 5 ml (1 teaspoon) ground cumin
- 1 seeded jalapeño pepper
- 300 ml (1 1/4 cups) chicken stock
- 125 ml (1/2 cup) tomato sauce
- 3/4 cup (190 mL) canned black kidney beans
- 30 ml (2 tablespoons) finely chopped parsley
- 1 lime
- Salt and pepper, to taste

Preparation

1. In a saucepan, melt the butter and add the onion. Simmer.
2. Add the rice and ground cumin. Continue cooking for about 2 minutes. Add the Jalapeno pepper. Deglaze with chicken stock and season.
3. Add the tomato sauce — cover and cook over medium heat for about 12 minutes.
4. When the rice is cooked, add the black beans and parsley. Continue cooking for minutes.
5. Add lime juice, salt, pepper, and serve.

149. Easy Baked Shepherd Pie

Ingredients

- 500 grams of freshly ground duck meat
- 3 tablespoons oil or olive oil
- 1 small onion, finely chopped
- 1 tsp ready-made garlic and salt seasoning
- 1 tablespoon dry spice chimichurri
- 4 medium cooked and mashed potatoes
- 1 tablespoon full of butter
- 100 ml of milk
- 25 grams of grated Parmesan cheese
- 1 pinch of salt

Preparation

1. In a pan heat oil, onion, and fry.
2. Add the meat and garlic and salt seasoning.
3. Fry well until the accumulated meat water dries.
4. After the meat is fried, add enough water to cover the meat.
5. Let it cook with the pan without a lid until the water almost dries again.
6. Add the chimichurri, stir and cook until the water dries, and the meat is fried until well dried.
7. Put the meat in an ovenproof dish and set aside.

8. Prepare a mash by mixing the remaining ingredients and spread over the meat.
9. Bake for about 20 minutes or until flushed.
10. Remove and serve.

150. Fish in the herb, garlic, and tomato sauce

Ingredients

- 6 teeth garlic peeled and whole
- 300 grams of halved mini onion
- 300 grams of halved pear (or cherry) tomato
- 1 packet of herbs (basil, parsley, and thyme) coarsely chopped
- 1/2 cup of olive oil
- 1 merluza fillet
- 2 cups wheat flour
- 3 egg
- 3 cups cornmeal
- black pepper to taste
- frying oil
- salt to taste

Preparation

1. In a large baking dish, place the garlic, onion, tomato, and herbs. Mix the olive oil, salt, and pepper.
2. Wrap the fish fillets and cover them with plastic wrap.
3. Refrigerate and marinate for 1 hour.
4. Remove the fish fillets, pass in the flour, then in the eggs beaten with a little salt and last in the cornmeal. Refrigerate.
5. Put the baking sheet with the marinade in the oven, preheated to 200 ° C, and let it bake for about 20 minutes.

6. Remove the breaded fillets from the refrigerator and fry them in hot oil until golden brown.
7. Serve the fish with the sauce in the baking dish.

151. Hot Salad with Kale and White Beans

Ingredients:

- 1 large bunch of kale well washed
- 1-2 tablespoons olive oil
- 1 stem of fresh rosemary, with the leaves removed from the stem and cut
- 1 small onion, cut
- 1 large carrot, sliced
- ½ teaspoon finely grated lemon zest
- 1 clove garlic, minced
- Salt to taste
- 2 cups cooked lima beans or other white beans plus cooking broth or 1 can (14 ounces)
- 1 cup plain parsley, cut
- Extra virgin olive oil, to spray
- Juice from ½ to small lemon, to spray (optional)

Preparation

1. Remove the leaves from the kale stalks. Cut into bite-sized pieces. Set aside.
2. Drain the white beans, reserving their broth. If you use canned beans, drain and wash. Set aside.
3. In a large pot, heat the oil over medium-high heat until it starts to boil. Add the rosemary, reserving a teaspoon, let it boil for

a moment, and then add the chopped onion, carrot, and lemon zest. Mix well and reduce the temperature. Cover and "sweat" the vegetables for minutes or until they are soft and the onion is a little golden, occasionally stirring to make sure they do not stick or burn.

4. Increase the temperature to medium-high. Add the cut garlic, stir and cook for 5 minutes. Add the cut greens with a good pinch of salt and sauté until they begin to wilt and soften.
5. Add ½ cup of the bean or water broth. Bring to a boil, lower the temperature for 10 to 15 minutes, or until the greens are soft and the liquid has evaporated. Put a little more broth or water if the vegetables seem very dry.
6. Mix the chopped parsley and the remaining teaspoon of rosemary, cook for 1 minute, then add the beans to the pot. Mix carefully with the greens. Try the seasoning.
7. Put off the burner and let the quinoa stand covered for 5 minutes. Serve sprinkled with a little olive oil and some lemon juice.

152. Scallion Swordfish

Ingredients

- 800 g of swordfish
- 1 lemon (medium)
- 1 dl of olive oil
- 2 Onions
- 1 dl of White Wine
- 1 c. (dessert) chopped parsley
- 4 royal gala apples
- 1 c. (soup) Butter
- 150 g chives
- Salt q.s.
- Paprika q.s.
- Salsa q.s.

Preparation

1. Season the swordfish slices with salt and lemon juice. Let them marinate for 30 minutes. After this time, fry them in olive oil. Add the peeled and sliced onions to half-moons and let them sauté.
2. Cool with white wine and season with a little more salt. Sprinkle with chopped parsley. Peel the apples cut them into

wedges and sauté them in butter. Peel the spring onions and add them to the fruit.
3. Season with some salt and paprika. Serve the fish topped with the spring onions and accompanied with the sauteed apple and spring onions. Garnish with parsley.

153. Easy Zucchini Spaghetti

INGREDIENTS

- 2 zucchinis
- 1 tablespoon olive oil
- 1 tablespoon butter
- 1/2 onion
- 1 teaspoon salt

SAUCE:

- 1 can of peeled tomatoes
- 3 tablespoons olive oil
- 1 clove of garlic
- 1/2 onion
- 1 teaspoon salt
- 1 tablespoon sugar
- black pepper to taste
- 2 tablespoons butter

INSTRUCTIONS

- Pass the zucchinis through a Julienne cutter, scorning only the seeded part.
- In a skillet, heat the oil and butter and add the onion.
- Add zucchini and sauté over low heat.
- Season with salt and set aside.

SAUCE:

- In a blender, beat the peeled tomatoes.
- In a pan, heat the olive oil and add the garlic clove and onion.
- Add the beaten tomatoes, salt, sugar and black pepper to taste.
- Stir well and when it boils, add the butter.
- Stir again to make the butter melt.
- Remove onion and garlic and serve with zucchini spaghetti.

154. Cauliflower Rice

INGREDIENTS

- 700 g of clean cauliflower separated in bouquets
- 1/2 tablespoon olive oil
- 1/2 tbsp chopped garlic
- 1/2 cup minced onion (80 g)
- 3/4 cup of boiling water
- salt to taste

INSTRUCTIONS

- In a processor, place 700g of clean cauliflower separately in bouquets and pulse until rice grain looks.
- In a saucepan over medium heat put 1/2 tbsp olive oil and sauté 1/2 tbsp chopped garlic and 1/2 tsp chopped onion for about 2 minutes.
- Add the processed cauliflower, 3/4 cup of boiling salted water to taste.
- Cover the pan, lower the heat and simmer for 10 minutes or until the water has dried.
- Serve immediately.

155. Salmon With Capers Sauce

INGREDIENTS

- 1 piece of 1 kg salmon
- 1 clove garlic
- Olive oil, lemon juice, rosemary, salt to taste
- Precooked potato slices
- Sauce:
- 1 tablespoon butter
- 2 tbsp olive oil
- 4 tbsp capers
- Parsley to taste

INSTRUCTIONS

- Season the salmon with lemon juice, garlic, rosemary, and salt.
- Let stand in refrigerator for 30 minutes.
- In a greased dish place the potato slices, the salmon.
- Drizzle with olive oil and bake for 30 minutes covered with aluminum foil.
- Remove the paper and let it brown.

SAUCE:

- In a skillet heat the butter and olive oil, place the drained and washed capers (they are very salty) and the parsley.
- Remove the salmon from the oven.
- Cover with sauce and serve.

156. Bacon Cupcake

INGREDIENTS

- thinly sliced bacon
- 6 eggs
- salt to taste
- black pepper to taste
- diced cheddar cheese to taste
- green smell to taste

INSTRUCTIONS

- Line cupcake pans with very thin slices of bacon - cover the bottom and sides of the pans.
- Bake at 210 ° C for 10 minutes to brown.
- When removing the pans from the oven, place 1 whole egg in each one over the bacon slices.
- Season with salt and black pepper to taste.
- Over the eggs, place cheddar cheese cubes to taste.
- Bake again at 230 ° C for 15 to 20 minutes.
- Remove from oven, finish with minced green-smelling and serve.

157. Chicken With Okra

INGREDIENTS

- 5 thighs
- 1 lemon juice
- 5 cloves minced garlic
- salt to taste
- black pepper to taste
- 1 + 1/4 cup oil
- 1 kg chopped okra
- 1 chopped onion
- 2 bay leaves
- 2 tbsp tomato sauce
- green smell to taste
- salt to taste

INSTRUCTIONS

- Arrange the drumsticks on a platter and season with 1 lemon juice, garlic, salt, and black pepper to taste.
- Cover the platter with plastic wrap and set aside in the refrigerator for 30 minutes.
- In a skillet, heat 1 cup of oil.
- Add the okra and saute to drool out.

- Remove the okra and place it on a plate with paper towels to drain.
- In another pan, heat 1/4 cup oil and fry the drumsticks.
- Remove the thighs and add the chopped onion and bay leaf to the pan, sauté well.
- Return the drumsticks to the pan and add the tomato sauce.
- Cover with hot water and cook for 20 minutes.
- Add the okra, the green smell and set the salt.

158. Green Salad With Chicken

INGREDIENTS

- 1 unit of romaine lettuce
- 1 cup of croutons

CHICKEN

- 250 g chicken breast
- salt to taste
- black pepper to taste
- 1 strand of olive oil

SAUCE

- 1 lemon juice
- 1 teaspoon mustard
- 1 teaspoon of English sauce
- 30 g of grated Parmesan
- 2 garlic cloves
- salt to taste
- black pepper to taste
- 200 ml olive oil

INSTRUCTIONS

- Season the chicken breast with salt and black pepper.
- Cook the chicken breast in a skillet with 1 trickle of olive oil.
- Slice the chicken breast and set aside.

SAUCE:

- Mix in a blender: lemon juice, mustard, English sauce, grated Parmesan, garlic, salt, and black pepper.
- Beat well and keep adding olive oil until emulsified.
- Wash the lettuce and serve with the chicken breast, croutons, and sauce.

159. Baked Eggplant

INGREDIENTS

- 2 eggplants
- salt to taste
- 2 tomatoes
- 1 large onion
- 3 tablespoons olive oil
- oregano to taste
- 4 cloves of mashed garlic
- salt to taste

INSTRUCTIONS

- Cut the eggplant into thin strips.
- Season with salt to taste.
- Cut the tomatoes and onions into slices.
- In a bowl add olive oil, oregano and mashed garlic.
- Mix well and season with salt.
- Dip this sauce into the bottom of a serving dish and arrange the first layer of eggplant.
- On top, put onions, tomatoes and more sauce.
- Repeat the process two more times.
- Cover with grated mozzarella and bake (180 ° C) for about 20 minutes.

160. Baked Fish Fillet

INGREDIENTS

- 500 g of fish fillet (tilapia, saint peter or other)
- 4 large potatoes peeled in 0.5 cm thick slices
- 2 chopped tomatoes
- 1/2 bell pepper (if it is large)
- 1 medium diced onion
- 1 tablespoon full of capers
- green smell to taste
- coriander to taste (optional)
- 1/2 tablespoon salt
- 1 clove garlic (small) well squeezed
- olive oil to taste

INSTRUCTIONS

- Season the fish fillet with salt and garlic and set aside.
- Mix the tomatoes, onions, peppers and capers and season with a little salt and add the green and coriander smell. Reserve.
- Grease a refractory with olive oil, and line with the raw potatoes.

- Cover the potatoes with the fish and spread over the tomato mixture. Drizzle with plenty of olive oil and bake for about 30 to 40 minutes.
- When you dry the liquid that accumulates in the bottom of the pan when it is baking and is golden brown is ready.
- Serve with integral or white rice, it's delicious!

161. Low Carb Chicken Quiche

INGREDIENTS

- 3 eggs
- 1 tbsp grated Parmesan cheese
- 200 g of grated mozzarella cheese
- 1 pot plain nonfat yogurt
- 300 g of shredded chicken
- 1 large chopped tomato
- Garlic and onion
- Light catchup

INSTRUCTIONS

- Preheat oven to 180°C.
- Sauté the shredded chicken with 1 chopped tomato, garlic, onion, light ketchup and salt to taste (this is a suggestion, you can sauté as you prefer). Reserve.
- Beat eggs with a tablespoon of grated cheese.
- Add the braised chicken, beaten eggs, yogurt and grated mozzarella on a platter and mix well.
- Bake for about 35 minutes.

162. Baked Eggplant Salad

INGREDIENTS

- 3 eggplants
- 1 green pepper
- 1 red bell pepper
- 1 yellow pepper
- 1 large onion
- 1/2 cup olive oil
- 1/4 cup of vinegar
- 3 tablespoons chopped black olives
- 2 cloves (large) minced garlic
- 1 bay leaf
- 2 tbsp oregano
- 2 tbsp chopped parsley
- salt to taste

INSTRUCTIONS

- Remove some of the eggplant's peel, cut into thin slices lengthwise and then cut into strips.
- Soak the sliced eggplants in salted water for half an hour, then rinse the salt and squeeze.

- Cut the onion and bell pepper into strips, put in a baking dish, add the eggplant, garlic, bay leaf, parsley, oregano, olive, and salt.
- Drizzle with half the vinegar and bake in a medium preheated oven for 45 minutes.
- Remove from oven and drizzle with olive oil and remaining vinegar.
- Let cool and serve.

163. Fish in tomato sauce

INGREDIENTS

- 4 frozen white fish fillets of your choice
- 2 cups cherry tomatoes cut in half
- 2 finely sliced garlic cloves
- 120 ml light chicken broth
- 60 ml of dry white wine (or use more chicken stock)
- 1/2 teaspoon salt
- 1/2 teaspoon black pepper
- 1/4 cup finely chopped fresh basil leaves (to garnish)

PREPARATION

1. Place the tomatoes, garlic, salt, and pepper in a pan over medium heat. Cook for 5 minutes or until tomatoes are soft.
2. Add chicken broth, white wine (if used), frozen fish fillets, and chopped basil. Cover and simmer 20-25 minutes, until the fish is fully cooked.
3. Finally, sprinkle with an additional handful of chopped basil and serve on a bed of rice, couscous or quinoa, if desired.

   Note: Thick white fish fillets such as cod, halibut, catfish, or mahi-mahi work best for this recipe.

164. Sea Bass and Peppers Salad

INGREDIENTS

- Seabass was very clean: A fillet of 150 g.
- Assorted lettuces: 100 g.
- Chives: To taste
- Fresh or roasted red pepper: 1
- Cherry tomatoes To taste
- Garlic clove and parsley 1
- Leek 1
- Carrot 1
- Olive oil One tablespoon
- Salt and lemon to taste

DIRECTIONS

4. We put the fillet of sea bass in aluminum foil. In the mortar, chop the garlic and parsley, add 2 small teaspoons of oil and cover the fillet of sea bass with it.
5. We also put some leek and carrot strips on the sea bass fillet (the vegetable ribbons can be made with the fruit peeler) and a little salt. Now we close the foil tightly and take it into the oven at 120 °C for 8-10 minutes. Once cooked, let it cool.

6. In a salad bowl, we put the lettuce mixture and chop the chives and pepper very finely. We add it too. Add the cherry tomatoes cut into quarters. Add only a small teaspoon of olive oil, salt, and lemon as a dressing and stir well and now add the fish with the vegetables that we have cooked in the oven and ready to eat.

165. Mexican baked beans and rice

INGREDIENTS

- 5 ml (1 teaspoon) unsalted butter
- 1 chopped yellow onion
- 3/4 cup (190 mL) basmati rice
- 5 ml (1 teaspoon) ground cumin
- 1 seeded jalapeño pepper
- 300 ml (1 1/4 cups) chicken stock
- 125 ml (1/2 cup) tomato sauce
- 3/4 cup (190 mL) canned black kidney beans
- 30 ml (2 tablespoons) finely chopped parsley
- 1 lime
- Salt and pepper, to taste

PREPARATION

6. In a saucepan, melt the butter and add the onion. Simmer.
7. Add the rice and ground cumin. Continue cooking for about 2 minutes. Add the Jalapeno pepper. Deglaze with chicken stock and season.
8. Add the tomato sauce — cover and cook over medium heat for about 12 minutes.

9. When the rice is cooked, add the black beans and parsley. Continue cooking for minutes.
10. Add lime juice, salt, pepper, and serve.

166. Easy Baked Shepherd Pie

INGREDIENTS

- 500 grams of freshly ground duck meat
- 3 tablespoons oil or olive oil
- 1 small onion, finely chopped
- 1 tsp ready-made garlic and salt seasoning
- 1 tablespoon dry spice chimichurri
- 4 medium cooked and mashed potatoes
- 1 tablespoon full of butter
- 100 ml of milk
- 25 grams of grated Parmesan cheese
- 1 pinch of salt

PREPARATION

- In a pan heat oil, onion, and fry.
- Add the meat and garlic and salt seasoning.
- Fry well until the accumulated meat water dries.
- After the meat is fried, add enough water to cover the meat.
- Let it cook with the pan without a lid until the water almost dries again.

- Add the chimichurri, stir and cook until the water dries, and the meat is fried until well dried.
- Put the meat in an ovenproof dish and set aside.
- Prepare a mash by mixing the remaining ingredients and spread over the meat.
- Bake for about 20 minutes or until flushed.
- Remove and serve.

167. Fish in the herb, garlic, and tomato sauce

INGREDIENTS

- 6 teeth garlic peeled and whole
- 300 grams of halved mini onion
- 300 grams of halved pear (or cherry) tomato
- 1 packet of herbs (basil, parsley, and thyme) coarsely chopped
- 1/2 cup of olive oil
- 1 merluza fillet
- 2 cups wheat flour
- 3 egg
- 3 cups cornmeal
- black pepper to taste
- frying oil
- salt to taste

PREPARATION

- In a large baking dish, place the garlic, onion, tomato, and herbs. Mix the olive oil, salt, and pepper.
- Wrap the fish fillets and cover them with plastic wrap.
- Refrigerate and marinate for 1 hour.
- Remove the fish fillets, pass in the flour, then in the eggs beaten with a little salt and last in the cornmeal. Refrigerate.

- Put the baking sheet with the marinade in the oven, preheated to 200 ° C, and let it bake for about 20 minutes.
- Remove the breaded fillets from the refrigerator and fry them in hot oil until golden brown.
- Serve the fish with the sauce in the baking dish.

168. Hot Salad with Kale and White Beans

INGREDIENTS:

- 1 large bunch of kale well washed
- 1-2 tablespoons olive oil
- 1 stem of fresh rosemary, with the leaves removed from the stem and cut
- 1 small onion, cut
- 1 large carrot, sliced
- ½ teaspoon finely grated lemon zest
- 1 clove garlic, minced
- Salt to taste
- 2 cups cooked lima beans or other white beans plus cooking broth or 1 can (14 ounces)
- 1 cup plain parsley, cut
- Extra virgin olive oil, to spray
- Juice from ½ to small lemon, to spray (optional)

PREPARATION

- Remove the leaves from the kale stalks. Cut into bite-sized pieces. Set aside.
- Drain the white beans, reserving their broth. If you use canned beans, drain and wash. Set aside.
- In a large pot, heat the oil over medium-high heat until it starts to boil. Add the rosemary, reserving a teaspoon, let it boil for

a moment, and then add the chopped onion, carrot, and lemon zest. Mix well and reduce the temperature. Cover and "sweat" the vegetables for minutes or until they are soft and the onion is a little golden, occasionally stirring to make sure they do not stick or burn.

- Increase the temperature to medium-high. Add the cut garlic, stir and cook for 5 minutes. Add the cut greens with a good pinch of salt and sauté until they begin to wilt and soften.
- Add ½ cup of the bean or water broth. Bring to a boil, lower the temperature for 10 to 15 minutes, or until the greens are soft and the liquid has evaporated. Put a little more broth or water if the vegetables seem very dry.
- Mix the chopped parsley and the remaining teaspoon of rosemary, cook for 1 minute, then add the beans to the pot. Mix carefully with the greens. Try the seasoning.
- Put off the burner and let the quinoa stand covered for 5 minutes. Serve sprinkled with a little olive oil and some lemon juice.

169. Scallion Swordfish

INGREDIENTS

- 800 g of swordfish
- 1 lemon (medium)
- 1 dl of olive oil
- 2 Onions
- 1 dl of White Wine
- 1 c. (dessert) chopped parsley
- 4 royal gala apples
- 1 c. (soup) Butter
- 150 g chives
- Salt q.s.
- Paprika q.s.
- Salsa q.s.

PREPARATION

4. Season the swordfish slices with salt and lemon juice. Let them marinate for 30 minutes. After this time, fry them in olive oil. Add the peeled and sliced onions to half-moons and let them sauté.
5. Cool with white wine and season with a little more salt. Sprinkle with chopped parsley. Peel the apples cut them into

wedges and sauté them in butter. Peel the spring onions and add them to the fruit.

6. Season with some salt and paprika. Serve the fish topped with the spring onions and accompanied with the sauteed apple and spring onions. Garnish with parsley.

170. Jambalaya Rice Recipe (also simply called Jambalaya)

INGREDIENTS

- 2 cups of needled rice
- 200 g boneless, skinless chicken meat, diced
- 200 g of thinly diced ham
- 1 medium onion, finely chopped
- 2 cloves garlic, minced
- 4 peeled, seedless tomatoes, chopped
- 1 stalk of chopped celery
- 1/2 diced red bell pepper
- 4 teaspoon chicken or shrimp background
- 2 tbsp tomato extract
- 2 tbsp butter
- 1/2 cup chopped green onions
- QB of salt
- 350 g of clean gray shrimp
- 1 lemon
- QB of freshly ground black pepper

Homemade Cajun Seasoning to taste

- 1 tsp garlic powder
- 1 tablespoon onion powder

- 1 tsp white ground pepper
- 1 tsp ground black pepper
- 1 teaspoon dried pepperoni pepper
- 1 tablespoon dry thyme
- 1 tablespoon dried oregano
- 1 tbsp spicy paprika
- 1 tablespoon dried tarragon
- 1 teaspoon ground cinnamon
- 1 teaspoon chili powder
- 1 tablespoon salt
- PS; add all ingredients and process or mash in the pestle.

PREPARATION

- Season the prawns with lemon juice, salt, and ground pepper. Let it taste for 30 minutes. Reserve
- In a pan, melt the butter with a little olive oil and brown the chicken cubes. Reserve
- In the pan, fat sauté the onion and garlic until it withers.
- Add celery, peppers, and tomatoes, and sauté for 2 minutes.
- Add the rice and sauté; Add tomato extract and chicken or shrimp background.
- Mix well and add the homemade Cajun spice to taste; Cook for 15 minutes over low heat, covered, without stirring.

- Add the reserved shrimp and cook another 5 minutes or until well-dried, mixing slightly.
- Remove from heat, sprinkle with green onions and serve very hot

171. Chick Curry (Thai Chicken)

INGREDIENTS

- 2 skinless, boneless chicken breasts (not too small)
- 3 tablespoons olive oil
- 1 small onion, finely chopped
- 2 cloves garlic, minced
- 3 tablespoons curry powder
- 1 teaspoon ground cinnamon
- 1 teaspoon paprika
- 1 bay leaf
- 1/2 teaspoon freshly grated ginger root
- 1 tbsp tomato extract
- 1 bottle of coconut milk
- 1/2 lemon (juice)
- 1 red bell pepper
- 1 cup pineapple (optional)

PREPARATION

- In a bowl season the chicken cubes with salt and lemon juice and set aside.
- Put in a pan the olive oil, garlic, onion, and saute until golden brown.
- Then put the chicken in the pan and saute until golden brown.

- Add pineapple (optional), curry, cinnamon, paprika, bay leaf, tomato extract, ginger, and red pepper. Saute for a few more minutes (if necessary, add a cup of water).
- Add coconut milk, cook for a few more minutes and serve.

172. Fried breaded lasagna with marinara sauce

INGREDIENTS

- 6 large slices of lasagna
- 1 cup of ricotta or cottage cheese
- 1 cup of mozzarella cheese
- 3 eggs
- ½ tablespoon of Italian seasoning
- 1 tablespoon of chopped parsley
- 1 clove of crushed garlic
- salt and pepper
- ¼ cup wheat flour
- c / n breadcrumbs
- c / n vegetable oil

DIRECTIONS

1. Cook in a large saucepan with water before the lasagna, according to the manufacturer's instructions.
2. Place the lasagna sheets on a previously greased baking sheet.
3. Combine ricotta cheese, mozzarella cheese, 1 egg, Italian seasoning, parsley, garlic and salt, and pepper to taste in a bowl. Incorporate all ingredients very well.

4. Distribute the previous mixture on each of the lasagna sheets and roll very well by pressing the filling.
5. To breach, pass each lasagna roll through bowls of flour, bowl with 2 beaten eggs, and to finish the dish with the breadcrumbs. Then enter the freezer for 30 minutes.
6. Heat plenty of oil in a deep pan. Introduce the lasagna rolls one by one and fry for 2 to 3 minutes. Place on the paper towel to remove excess oil.
7. Cut lasagna rolls in half and serve on a marinara sauce base.

Marinara sauce:

1. In a medium saucepan heat 2 tablespoons of oil, add 1 finely chopped onion and 1 clove of crushed garlic and brown for 5 minutes.
2. Stir with a wooden spoon to prevent burning. Add 2 cups of chopped tomato, 2 tablespoons of tomato paste, and 2 tablespoons of chopped fresh basil, ½ tablespoon of ground black pepper, 1 teaspoon of ground oregano and ½ tablespoon of salt.
3. Cook until the sauce boils. Put it on low heat and continue cooking for 20 minutes or until the sauce acquires a thick consistency.

173. Baked Mushrooms with Pumpkin And Chipotle Polenta

INGREDIENTS

- 900 g mix of mushrooms, such as maitake, jasmine ear and black shimeji - coarsely chopped - thinly sliced porcini crimini mushrooms - and coarsely chopped shiitakessem stalks
- About 1/3 cup of extra virgin olive oil
- 1 garlic head, crushed cloves
- A small handful of sage, finely chopped or sliced
- Sea salt and freshly ground black pepper.
- 1 cup cooked pumpkin puree
- 3 cups chicken broth
- Nutmeg, freshly grated
- 1 chipotle adobo sauce, seedless and finely chopped, plus a small spoon of adobo sauce
- 1 cup quick-cooking polenta
- 2 tbsp butter
- 2 tbsp honey
- Roasted seeds for decoration
- Chives, minced, for decoration

PREPARATION

1. Preheat the oven to 220 ºC.
2. Mix the mushrooms with extra virgin olive oil, garlic, brine, salt, and pepper and bake for 25 minutes.
3. Meanwhile, in a small pan, put it pumpkin puree over medium heat, along with some chicken broth to dilute.
4. Season with salt, pepper, and nutmeg.
5. In another pan, put the remaining stock and bring to a boil, then add the chipotle, adobo sauce, polenta and mix using a wire whisk. Continue beating the polenta until the sides are far from the pan walls, then add the butter, honey, and beat again.
6. Combine pumpkin and polenta and serve in individual shallow bowls.
7. Top with roasted mushrooms and Siva with roasted seeds and chives for garnish.

174. Cauliflower and Pumpkin Casserole

Ingredients

- 2 tbsp. olive oil
- 1/4 medium yellow onion, minced
- 6 cups chopped forage kale into small pieces (about 140 g)
- 1 little clove garlic, minced
- Salt and freshly ground black pepper
- 1/2 cup low sodium chicken broth
- 2 cups of 1.5 cm diced pumpkin (about 230 g)
- 2 cups of 1.5 cm diced zucchini (about 230 g)
- 2 tbsp. mayonnaise
- 3 cups frozen, thawed brown rice
- 1 cup grated Swiss cheese
- 1/3 cup grated Parmesan
- 1 cup panko flour
- 1 large beaten egg
- Cooking spray

Preparation

1. Preheat oven to 200 ° C. Heats the oil in a large nonstick skillet over medium heat. Add onions and cook, occasionally stirring, until browned and tender (about 5 minutes). Add the cabbage, garlic, and 1/2 teaspoon salt and 1/2 teaspoon pepper and cook until the cabbage is light (about 2 minutes).

2. Add the stock and continue to cook until the cabbage withers, and most of the stock evaporates (about 5 minutes). Add squash, zucchini, and 1/2 teaspoon salt and mix well. Continue cooking until the pumpkin begins to soften (about 8 minutes). Remove from heat and add mayonnaise.
3. In a bowl, combine cooked vegetables, brown rice, cheese, 1/2 cup flour, and large egg and mix well. Spray a 2-liter casserole with cooking spray. Spread the mixture across the bottom of the pan and cover with the remaining flour, 1/4 teaspoon salt and a few pinches of pepper. Bake until the squash and zucchini are tender and the top golden and crispy (about 35 minutes). Serve hot.

   Advance Preparation Tip: Freeze the casserole for up to 2 weeks. Cover with aluminum foil and heat at 180 ° C until warm (35 to 45 minutes).

175. Thai beef salad Tears of the Tiger

Ingredients

- 800 g of beef tenderloin
- For the marinade :
- 2 tablespoons of soy sauce
- 1 tablespoon soup of honey
- 1 pinch of the pepper mill
- For the sauce :
- 1 small bunch of fresh coriander
- 1 small bouquet of mint
- 3 tablespoons soup of fish sauce
- lemon green
- 1 clove of garlic
- tablespoons soup of sugar palm (or brown sugar)
- 1 bird pepper or ten drops of Tabasco
- 1 small glass of raw Thai rice to make grilled rice powder
- 200 g of arugula or young shoots of salad

Preparation

- Cut the beef tenderloin into strips and put it in a container. Sprinkle with 2 tablespoons soy sauce, 1 tablespoon honey, and pepper. Although soak thoroughly and let marinate 1 hour at room temperature.

- Meanwhile, prepare the roasted rice powder. Pour a glass of Thai rice into an anti-adhesive pan. Dry color the rice, constantly stirring to avoid burning. When it has a lovely color, get rid of it on a plate and let it cool.
- When it has cooled, reduce it to powder by mixing it with the robot.
- Wash and finely chop mint and coriander. Put in a container and add lime juice, chopped garlic clove, 3 tablespoons Nuoc mam, 3 tablespoons brown sugar, 3 tablespoons water, 1 tablespoon sauce soy, and a dozen drops of Tabasco. Mix well and let stand the time that the sugar melts and the flavors mix.
- Place a bed of salad on a dish. Cook the beef strips put them on the salad. Sprinkle with the spoonful of sauce and roasted rice powder. To be served as is or with a Thai cooked white rice scented.

176. Stuffed apples with shrimp

Ingredients

- 6 medium apples
- 1 lemon juice
- 2 tablespoons butter

Filling:

- 300 gr of shrimp
- 1 onion minced
- ½ cup chopped parsley
- 2 tbsp flour
- 1 can of cream/cream
- 100 gr of curd
- 1 tablespoon butter
- 1 tbsp pepper sauce
- Salt to taste

Preparation

- Cut a cap from each apple, remove the seeds a little from the pulp on the sides, and put the pulp in the bottom, but leaving a cavity.
- Pass a little lemon and some butter on the apples, bake them in the oven. Remove from oven, let cool and bring to freeze.

- Prepare the shrimp sauce in a pan by mixing the butter with the flour, onion, parsley, and pepper sauce.
- Then add the prawn shrimp to the sauce. When boiling, mix the cream cheese and sour cream.
- Stuff each apple. Serve hot or cold, as you prefer.

177. A Quick Recipe of Grilled Chicken Salad with Oranges

Ingredients:

- 75 ml (1/3 cup) orange juice
- 30 ml (2 tablespoons) lemon juice
- 45 ml (3 tablespoons) of extra virgin olive oil
- 15 ml (1 tablespoon) Dijon mustard
- 2 cloves of garlic, chopped
- 1 ml (1/4 teaspoon) salt, or as you like
- Freshly ground pepper to your taste
- 1 lb. (450 g) skinless chicken breast, trimmed
- 25 g (1/4 cup) pistachio or flaked almonds, toasted
- 600 g (8c / 5 oz) of mesclun, rinsed and dried
- 75 g (1/2 cup) minced red onion
- 2 medium oranges, peeled, quartered and sliced

Preparation:

- Place the orange juice, lemon juice, oil, mustard, garlic, salt, and pepper in a small bowl or jar with an airtight lid; whip or shake to mix. Reserve 75 milliliters (1/3 cup) of this salad vinaigrette and 45 milliliters (three tablespoons) for basting.
- Place the rest of the vinaigrette in a shallow glass dish or resealable plastic bag. Add the chicken and turn it over to coat.

Cover or close and marinate in the refrigerator for at least 20 minutes or up to two hours.

- Preheat the barbecue over medium heat. Lightly oil the grill by rubbing it with a crumpled paper towel soaked in oil (use the tongs to hold the paper towel). Remove the chicken from the marinade and discard the marinade. Grill the chicken 10 to 15 centimeters (four to six inches) from the heat source, basting the cooked sides with the basting vinaigrette, until it is no longer pink in the center, and Instant-read thermometer inserted in the thickest part records 75 ° C (170 ° F), four to six minutes on each side. Transfer the chicken to a cutting board and let it rest for five minutes.
- Meanwhile, grill almonds (or pistachios) in a small, dry pan on medium-low heat, stirring constantly, until lightly browned, about two to three minutes. Transfer them to a bowl and let them cool.
- Place the salad and onion mixture in a large bowl. Mix with the vinaigrette reserved for the salad. Divide the salad into four plates. Slice chicken and spread on salads. Sprinkle orange slices on top and sprinkle with pistachios (or almonds).

178. Red Curry with Vegetable

Ingredients

- 600 g sweet potatoes
- 200 g canned chickpeas
- 2 leek whites
- 2 tomatoes
- 100 g of spinach shoots
- 40 cl of coconut milk
- 1 jar of Greek yogurt
- 1 lime
- 3 cm fresh ginger
- 1 small bunch of coriander
- 1/2 red onion
- 2 cloves garlic
- 4 tbsp. red curry paste
- salt

Preparation

- Peel the sweet potatoes and cut them into pieces. Clean the leek whites and cut them into slices. Peel and seed the tomatoes.
- Mix the Greek yogurt with a drizzle of lime juice, chopped onion, salt, and half of the coriander leaves.

- In a frying pan, heat 15 cl of coconut milk until it reduces and forms a multitude of small bubbles. Brown curry paste with chopped ginger and garlic.
- Add vegetables, drained chickpeas, remaining coconut milk, and salt. Cook for 20 min covered, then 5 min without lid for the sauce to thicken.
- When serving, add spinach sprouts and remaining coriander. Serve with the yogurt sauce.

179. Baked Turkey Breast with Cranberry Sauce

Ingredients

- 2 kilos of whole turkey breast
- 1 tablespoon olive oil
- 1/4 cup onion
- 2 cloves of garlic
- thyme
- poultry seasonings
- you saved
- coarse-grained salt
- 2 butter spoons
- 1/4 cup minced echallot
- 1/4 cup chopped onion
- 1 clove garlic
- 2 tablespoons flour
- 1 1/2 cups of blueberries
- 2 cups apple cider
- 2 tablespoons maple honey
- peppers

Preparation

1. Grind in the blender ¼ cup onion, 2 garlic with herbs. Add 1 tablespoon of oil and spread the breast with this.

2. Put in the baking tray, add a cup of citron and bake at 350 Fahrenheit (180 ° C) to have a thermometer record 165 Fahrenheit (75 ° C) inside, about an hour, add ½ cup of water if necessary.
3. Bring the citron to a boil, add the blueberries, and leave a few minutes. In the butter (2 tablespoons), acitronar the onion (1/4 cup), echallot, and garlic (1 clove).
4. Add the flour to the onion and echallot and leave a few minutes. Add the citron, cranberries, and honey and leave on low heat. Season with salt and pepper, let the blueberries are soft, go to the processor, and if you want to strain.
5. Return to the fire and let it thicken slightly.
6. Slice the thin turkey breast and serve with the blueberry sauce.

180. Oatmeal and berry muffins

INGREDIENTS

- 1 cup (250 mL) non-blanched all-purpose flour
- ½ cup (125 mL) quick-cooking oatmeal 1/2 cup
- (160 mL) stuffed brown sugar
- 1/2 tbsp (1/2 cup) tea) baking soda
- 2 eggs
- 125 ml (1/2 cup) applesauce
- 60 ml (1/4 cup)
- orange canola oil 1, grated rind only
- 1 lemon, grated rind
- 15 ml (1 tbsp) lemon juice
- 180 ml (3/4 cup) fresh raspberries (see note)
- 180 ml (3/4 cup) fresh or blueberries (or blackberries)

PREPARATION

1. Put the grill at the center of the oven. Preheat oven to 180 ° C (350 ° F). Line 12 muffin cups with paper or silicone trays.
2. In a bowl, combine flour, oatmeal, brown sugar, and baking soda. Book.

3. In a big bowl, whisk together eggs, applesauce, oil, citrus zest, and lemon juice. Add the dry ingredients to the wooden spoon. Add the berries and mix gently.
4. Spread the mixture in the boxes. Sprinkle top with pistachio muffins. Bake for 20 to 22 minutes or until a toothpick inserted in the center of a muffin comes out clean. Let cool.

181. Crunchy Blueberry and Apples

INGREDIENTS

Crunchy

- 1 cup (1¼ cup) quick-cooking oatmeal
- ¼ cup (60 mL) brown sugar
- ¼ cup (60 mL) unbleached all-purpose flour
- 90 ml (6 tablespoons) melted margarine

Garnish

- 125 ml (½ cup) brown sugar
- 20 ml (4 teaspoons) cornstarch
- 1 liter (4 cups) fresh or frozen blueberries (not thawed)
- 500 ml (2 cups) grated apples
- 1 Tbsp.
- (15 mL) melted margarine 15 mL (1 tablespoon) lemon juice

PREPARATION

1. Put the grill at the center of the oven. Preheat oven to 180 ° C (350 ° F).
2. In a bowl, mix dry ingredients. Add the margarine and mix until the mixture is just moistened. Book.
3. In a 20-cm (8-inch) square baking pan, combine brown sugar and cornstarch. Add the fruits, margarine, lemon juice, and

mix well. Cover with crisp and bake between 55 minutes and 1 hour, or until the crisp is golden brown. Serve warm or cold.

182. Fresh Cranberry Pie

INGREDIENTS

- 1 ½ cup crumbled Graham crackers
- ¼ cup salt-free chopped pecans
- 1 ¾ cup Splenda Sweetener
- ½ cup non-hydrogenated salt-free margarine
- 1 ½ cup freshly picked cranberries
- 2 egg whites
- 1 tbsp. thawed apple juice concentrate
- 1 tbsp. vanilla extract
- 1 liter Cool Whip Whipped Topping, thawed

Cranberry Frosting:

- ¼ cup Splenda Sweetener
- ¼ cup caster sugar
- 1 Tbsp. cornstarch
- ¾ cup fresh cranberries
- ¾ cup of water

PREPARATION

1. Preheat oven to 375 ° F (190 ° C).

2. Mix crumbled crackers, pecans, and ¾ cup of Splenda. Add the margarine, mix well, and arrange on a hinged mold pressing on the bottom and the sides. Bake dough for 6 minutes or until slightly browned, let cool.
3. Mix the cranberries with 1 cup of Splenda. Let stand for 5 minutes. Add the egg whites, apple juice, and vanilla. Beat at low speed until foamy, and then beat at high speed for 5 to 8 minutes until mixture is firm.
4. Stir in the whipped topping in the cranberry mixture. Pour the mixture over the pre-cooked dough. Refrigerate at least 4 hours until the mixture is firm.
5. To make the icing, mix the sugar, Splenda, and cornstarch in a saucepan. Stir in cranberries and water. Cook, stirring until bubbles appear. Continue cooking, occasionally stirring until cranberry skin comes off. Use the mixture at room temperature. Do not refrigerate: the sauce may crystallize and become opaque.
6. Remove the tart from the pan and arrange on a serving platter, using a spoon, coat with icing.

183. Low carb chocolate mousse

INGREDIENTS

- 300 ml whipping cream
- ½ tsp vanilla extract
- 2 egg yolks
- 1 pinch salt
- 100 g dark chocolate with a minimum of 80% cocoa solids

INSTRUCTIONS

- Break or cut the chocolate into small pieces. Melt in the microwave (at intervals of 20 seconds, stirring each time) or using a water bath. Reserve to cool to room temperature.
- Beat the cream until it is about to snow. Add the vanilla towards the end.
- Mix the egg yolks with the salt in a separate bowl.
- Add the melted chocolate to the yolks and mix until you have a uniform consistency dough.
- Add a couple of tablespoons of whipped cream to the chocolate mixture and stir to make it a little more liquid. Add the remaining cream and add it to the mixture.
- Divide the dough into ramekins or serving glasses. Put in the refrigerator and let cool for at least 2 hours. Serve alone or with fresh berries.

184. Chocolate Keto Cake with Peanut Butter Cream

INGREDIENTS

- 225 ml (110 g) ground almonds
- 175 ml (125 g) erythritol
- 125 ml (50 g) cocoa powder
- 1½ tbsp (12 g) psyllium powder husks
- 1 tbsp baking powder
- ¼ tsp Salt
- 4 eggs
- 225 g (225 ml) cream cheese
- 110 g melted salted butter
- Peanut Butter Frosting
- 225 g salted butter
- 225 g (225 ml) cream cheese
- 125 ml unsalted and unsweetened peanut butter
- 60 ml (50 g) erythritol, powder
- 2 tsp vanilla extract
- Ornaments
- 10 cherries (optional)
- 125 ml whipping cream
- 1 tbsp (10 g) salted peanuts, chopped

INSTRUCTIONS

- Place the rack in the center of the oven and preheat to 180 ° C (350 ° F).
- Mix almond flour, sweetener, cocoa powder (filter to remove lumps), ground psyllium husk powder, baking powder, and salt in a medium bowl. Beat until well mixed. Reserve.
- Pour the eggs into a large bowl. Beat with the electric pastry mixer for a couple of minutes until they are fluffy. Add cream cheese and melted butter. Continue beating until the mixture is smooth and homogeneous.
- Add the flour mixture in the bowl with the eggs and beat a couple of minutes until the cake dough is smooth.
- Grease two cake moulds 18 cm (7 inches), or do it one by one if you only have one mold. Pour half of the dough into each mold and distribute it evenly. Bake for 15-20 minutes or until a toothpick in the center comes out clean.
- Allow cooling for at least 10 minutes in the mold before passing it to a rack to cool. Wrap the layers with plastic wrap and place in the refrigerator; let cool completely, preferably overnight.

185. Low carb chocolate peanut squares

INGREDIENTS

- 100 g dark chocolate with a minimum of 70% cocoa solids
- 4 tbsp butter or coconut oil
- 1 pinch salt
- 60 ml of peanut butter
- ½ tsp vanilla extract
- 1 tsp powdered licorice or ground cardamom (green)
- 60 ml (35 g) chopped salted peanuts, for decoration

INSTRUCTIONS

- Melt the chocolate and butter or coconut oil in the microwave or in a water-bath pot. If you don't have a pot for a water bath, you can put a glass bowl on top of a pot with boiling water. Make sure the water does not reach the container. The chocolate will melt by the heat of the steam. Mix all other ingredients and pour the mixture into a small roasting pan lined with baking paper (no larger than 10 x 15 centimeters).
- Let cool for a while and cover with finely chopped peanuts or other creative toppings. Refrigerate.
- When the dough is ready, cut it into small squares with a sharp knife. Remember that all whims are small, not more than a square of 2.5 cm x 2.5 cm. Store in the refrigerator or freezer.

186. Eggplant and chickpea bites

INGREDIENTS

- 3 large aubergines cut in half (make a few cuts in the flesh with a knife) Spray
- oil
- 2 large cloves garlic, peeled and deglazed
- 2 tbsp. coriander powder
- 2 tbsp. cumin seeds
- 400 g canned chickpeas, rinsed and drained
- 2 Tbsp. chickpea flour
- Zest and juice of 1/2 lemon
- 1/2 lemon quartered for serving
- 3 tbsp. tablespoon of polenta

PREPARATION

- Heat the oven to 200°C (180°C rotating heat, gas level 6). Spray the eggplant halves generously with oil and place them on the meat side up on a baking sheet. Sprinkle with coriander and cumin seeds, and then place the cloves of garlic on the plate. Season and roast for 40 minutes until the flesh of eggplant is completely tender. Reserve and let cool a little.
- Scrape the flesh of the eggplant in a bowl with a spatula and throw the skins in the compost. Thoroughly scrape and make sure to incorporate spices and crushed roasted garlic. Add chickpeas, chickpea flour, zest, and lemon juice. Crush

roughly and mix well, check to season. Do not worry if the mixture seems a bit soft - it will firm up in the fridge.

- Form about twenty pellets and place them on a baking sheet covered with parchment paper. Let stand in the fridge for at least 30 minutes.
- Preheat oven to 180°C (rotating heat 160°C, gas level 4). Remove the meatballs from the fridge and coat them by rolling them in the polenta. Place them back on the baking sheet and spray a little oil on each. Roast for 20 minutes until golden and crisp. Serve with lemon wedges. You can also serve these dumplings with a spicy yogurt dip with harissa, this delicious but spicy mashed paste of hot peppers and spices from the Maghreb.

187. Baba Ghanouj

INGREDIENTS

- 1 large aubergine, cut in half lengthwise
- 1 head of garlic, unpeeled
- 30 ml (2 tablespoons) of olive oil
- Lemon juice to taste

PREPARATION

- Put the grill at the center of the oven. Preheat the oven to 350 ° F. Line a baking sheet with parchment paper.
- Place the eggplant on the plate, skin side up. Roast until the meat is very tender and detaches easily from the skin, about 1 hour depending on the size of the eggplant. Let cool.
- Meanwhile, cut the tip of the garlic cloves. Place the garlic cloves in a square of aluminum foil. Fold the edges of the sheet and fold together to form a tightly wrapped foil. Roast with the eggplant until tender, about 20 minutes. Let cool. Purée the pods with a garlic press.
- With a spoon, scoop out the flesh of the eggplant and place it in the bowl of a food processor. Add the garlic puree, the oil, and the lemon juice. Stir until purée is smooth and pepper.
- Serve with mini pita bread.

188. Spicy crab dip

INGREDIENTS

- 1 can of 8 oz softened cream cheese
- 1 tbsp. to . finely chopped onions
- 1 tbsp. at . lemon juice
- 2 tbsp. at . Worcestershire sauce
- 1/8 tsp. at t. black
- pepper Cayenne pepper to taste
- 2 tbsp. to s. of milk or non-fortified rice drink
- 1 can of 6 oz of crabmeat

PREPARATION

- Preheat the oven to 375 ° F (190 ° C).
- Pour the cream cheese into a bowl. Add the onions, lemon juice, Worcestershire sauce, black pepper, and cayenne pepper. Mix well. Stir in the milk/rice drink. Add the crabmeat and mix until you obtain a homogeneous mixture.
- Pour the mixture into a baking dish. Cook without covering for 15 minutes or until bubbles appear. Serve hot with low-sodium crackers or triangle cut pita bread. OR
- Microwave until bubbles appear, about 4 minutes, stirring every 1 to 2 minutes.

189. Potatoes" of Parmesan cheese

Ingredients

- 75 g grated Parmesan cheese
- 1 tbsp (8 g) Chia seeds
- 2 tbsp (20 g) whole flaxseeds
- 2½ tbsp (20 g) pumpkin seeds

Instructions

- Preheat the oven to 180 ° C (350 ° F).
- Cover a baking sheet with baking paper.
- Mix the cheese and seeds in a bowl.
- With a spoon, put small piles of the mixture on the baking paper, leaving some space between them. Do not flatten the piles. Bake for 8 to 10 minutes checks frequently. "Potatoes" should take a light brown color, but not dark brown.
- Remove from the oven and let cool before removing the "potatoes" from the paper and serve them.

190. Chili cheese chicken with crispy and delicious cabbage salad

INGREDIENTS

Chili Cheese Chicken

- 400 grams of chicken
- 200 grams of tomatoes
- 100 grams of cream cheese
- 125 grams of cheddar
- 40 grams of jalapenos
- 60 grams of bacon

Crispy Cabbage Salad

- 0.5 pcs casserole
- 200 grams of Brussels sprouts
- grams of almonds
- 3 paragraph mandarins
- 1 tablespoon olive oil
- 1 teaspoon apple cider vinegar
- 0.5 tsp salt
- 0.25 teaspoon pepper
- 1 tablespoon lemon

PREPARATION

- Turn on the oven at 200 °. Cut tomatoes in half and place in the bottom of a dish. Put chicken fillets in the dish, place half of the cream cheese on each chicken fillet and sprinkle with cheddar. Spread jalapenos in the dish and bake it first for 25 minutes. Place bacon on a baking sheet with baking paper, and bake it for 10 minutes. Next, make the cabbage salad. When the chicken dish has been given 35 minutes, it should be done
- Put the Brussels sprouts and cumin in a food processor and blend it well and thoroughly. Make the dressing of juice from one mandarin, olive oil, apple cider vinegar, salt, pepper, and lemon juice. Put the cabbage in a dish and spread the dressing over. Chop almonds, cut the tangerine into slices and place it on the salad.
- Sprinkle the bacon over the chicken dish before serving, and serve it with the cabbage salad!

191. KETO pumpkin pie for Halloween, sweet and spicy

INGREDIENTS

Pie Bottom

- 110 grams of almond flour
- 50 grams of sucrose
- 0.5 tsp salt
- grams of protein powder 1 scoop
- 1 paragraph eggs
- 80 grams of butter
- 15 grams of fiber

The Filling

- 1 pcs Hokkaido
- 3 paragraph egg yolks
- 60 ml of coconut milk the fat, not the water
- 1 teaspoon vanilla powder
- 15 grams of protein powder
- 1 teaspoon cinnamon
- grams of sucrose
- 0.5 tsp cardamom Bla
- 0.5 tsp cloves

PREPARATION

- Preheat oven to 175 °. Start making the bottom as it needs to be baked!
- Mix all the dry ingredients in a bowl and add the wet ones. Stir it well and take over with your hands so you can shape it into a lump. Take a piece of baking paper and place the dough lump. Place a piece of baking paper on top and flatten the dough. Shape it to the size of a regular pie mold 24 cm in diameter. Use a rolling pin if necessary. Prick holes in the bottom and behind dough in the oven for 8-10 minutes. Be careful about giving it too much (we did it the first time)
- Then make the filling. Cut the meat off your Hokkaido (or the garbage off the meat!) And cook it in a saucepan for 15-20 minutes. Put it in a food processor and add all the other ingredients and blend it well.
- Pour the stuffing into the baked pie and bake again for approx. 25-30 minutes more until it looks golden and done. Eat when cool or cool down first. A dollop of whipped cream is great too!

DINNER

192. Italian Keto Casserole

Ingredients

- 200 g Shirataki noodles
- 2 tbsp olive oil
- 1 small onion, diced
- 2 garlic cloves, finely chopped
- 1 tsp dried marjoram
- 450 g ground beef
- 1 tsp salt
- ½ tsp ground pepper
- 2 chopped tomatoes
- 1 cup of fat cream
- 340 g ricotta cheese
- ⅓ cup grated parmesan
- 1 egg
- ¼ cup parsley, roughly chopped

Cooking

- Preheat the oven to 190 degrees.
- Prepare the shirataki noodles as indicated on the packaging, strain well and set aside.
- Place a large non-stick pan over high heat. Add oil, onion, garlic, and marjoram, and fry for 2-3 minutes, until the onion is soft.

- Add ground beef, salt and pepper, and simmer, stirring, while the mixture is browned (if it is watery, drain the excess liquid).
- Add tomatoes and fat cream, and cook for 5 minutes.
- Remove from heat and mix with noodles. Transfer the mixture to a baking dish.
- In a small bowl, mix ricotta, parmesan, egg, and parsley. Spoon over the casserole.
- Bake 35-45 minutes until golden brown.

193. Salmon Keto Cutlets

Ingredients

- 450 g canned salmon
- ½ cup almond flour
- ¼ cup shallots, finely chopped
- 2 tbsp parsley, finely chopped
- 1 tbsp dried chopped onions
- 2 large eggs
- Zest of 1 lemon
- 1 clove garlic, finely chopped
- ½ tsp salt
- ½ tsp ground white pepper
- 3 tbsp olive oil

Cooking

- Put all the ingredients except the oil in a large bowl and mix well.
- Form 8 identical cutlets.
- Place a large non-stick pan over medium heat. Add half the butter.
- Fry salmon cutlets in portions, adding more oil as needed, for 2-3 minutes on each side.
- Serve the cutlets warm or cold with lemon wedges and low carbohydrate mayonnaise.

194. Brussels sprouts with maple syrup

Ingredients

- 2 tbsp olive oil
- 453.59 g Brussels sprouts, halved
- ½ tsp salt
- A pinch of ground black pepper
- 2 tbsp butter
- ½ cup pecans
- 2 tbsp sugarless maple syrup

Cooking

- Place a large non-stick pan over high heat and add olive oil.
- Put halves of cabbage in a pan with the cut side down, and sprinkle with salt and pepper.
- Fry for 3-4 minutes until brown and crispy, then turn over.
- Reduce heat to medium and add butter. Cook another 3 minutes.
- Add the pecans and mix.
- Once the cabbage is soft, add maple syrup without sugar. Throw the cabbage in a pan, and remove from heat.

195. Baked Cauliflower

Ingredients

- 1 medium cauliflower
- 113 g of salted butter
- ⅓ cup finely grated parmesan
- 3 tbsp Dijon mustard
- 2 minced garlic cloves
- Zest of 1 lemon
- ½ tsp salt
- ½ tsp ground pepper
- 28 g fresh Parmesan
- 1 tbsp finely chopped parsley

Cooking

- Preheat the oven to 190 degrees.
- Put the cauliflower in a small baking dish (I used a 9-inch).
- Put the remaining ingredients in a small saucepan, except for fresh parmesan and parsley, and put on low heat until they melt. Whip together.
- Lubricate cauliflower ⅓ of the oil mixture.
- Bake for 20 minutes, then remove from the oven and pour another quarter of the oil mixture.

- Bake for another 20 minutes and pour over the remaining oil mixture.
- Cook for another 20-30 minutes until the core is soft (check by inserting a small knife).
- Put on a plate, sprinkle a drop of oil from the mold, grate fresh parmesan and sprinkle with parsley.

196. Mushroom Risotto with Mushrooms

Recipe

- 2 tbsp olive oil
- 2 minced garlic cloves
- 1 small onion, finely diced
- 1 tsp salt
- ½ tsp ground white pepper
- 200 g chopped mushrooms
- ¼ cup chopped oregano leaves
- 255 g "rice" of cauliflower
- ¼ cup vegetable broth
- 2 tbsp butter
- ⅓ cup grated parmesan

Cooking

- Place a large non-stick pan over high heat.
- Add oil, garlic, onions, salt, and pepper, and sauté for 5-7 minutes until the onions become clear.
- Add mushrooms and oregano, and cook for 5 minutes.
- Add cauliflower rice and vegetable broth, then reduce heat to medium. Cook the risotto, stirring frequently, for 10-15 minutes, until the cauliflower is soft.
- Remove from heat, and mix with butter and parmesan.
- Try and add more seasoning if you want.

197. Low Carb Green Bean Casserole

Recipe

- 2 tbsp butter
- 1 small chopped onion
- 2 minced garlic cloves
- 226.8 g chopped mushrooms
- ½ tsp salt
- ½ tsp ground pepper
- ½ cup chicken stock
- ½ cup of fat cream
- ½ tsp xanthan gum
- 453.59 g green beans (with cut ends)
- 56.7 g crushed cracklings

Cooking

- Preheat the oven to 190 degrees.
- Add oil, onion, and garlic to a non-stick pan over high heat. Fry until onion is clear.
- Add mushrooms, salt, and pepper. Cook for 7 minutes until the mushrooms are tender.
- Add chicken stock and cream, and bring to a boil. Sprinkle with xanthan gum, mix and cook for 5 minutes.

- Add the string beans to the creamy mixture and pour it into the baking dish.
- Cover with foil and bake for 20 minutes.
- Remove the foil, sprinkle with greaves and bake for another 10-15 minutes.

198. French Zucchini (Gratin)

Recipe

- 2 tbsp butter or ghee ghee
- 2 garlic cloves, chopped
- 3 tbsp chopped fresh onions
- 125 g almond milk or heavy cream
- 226 g grated cheddar cheese
- 2 medium sliced zucchini

Cooking

- Melt the butter in a skillet over medium heat. Then add the garlic and onions, and cook until they are browned and fragrant.
- Add almond milk (or cream) and cook until it boils. Slowly add half the grated cheese and mix until it melts.
- Add chopped zucchini and mix well, covering the vegetables with the sauce. Cook another 5 minutes.
- Sprinkle the remaining cheese on top. Then bake in the oven at 204 ° C until the top is browned (about 20 minutes).

199. Avocado Low Carb Burger

Recipe

- 1 avocado
- 1 leaf lettuce
- 2 slices of prosciutto or any ham
- 1 slice of tomato
- 1 egg
- ½ tbsp olive oil for frying

For the sauce:

- 1 tbsp low carb mayonnaise
- ¼ tsp low carb hot sauce
- ¼ tsp mustard
- ¼ tsp Italian seasoning
- ½ tsp sesame seeds (optional

Cooking

- In a small bowl, combine keto-friendly mayonnaise, mustard, hot sauce, and Italian seasoning.
- Heat 1/2 tablespoon of olive oil in a pan and cook an egg. The yolk must be fluid.
- Cut the avocado in half, remove the peel and bone. Cut the narrowest part of the avocado so that the fruit can stand on a plate.

- Fill the hole in one half of the avocado with the prepared sauce.
- Top with lettuce, prosciutto strips, a slice of tomato and a fried egg.
- Cover with the other half of the avocado and sprinkle with sesame seeds (optional).

200. Italian sausages in a slow cooker with pepper

Recipe

- 283.5 g low-carb Italian sausages
- 1/2 chopped bell pepper
- 242 g canned tomatoes
- 1/2 chopped onion
- 1 clove of garlic
- 1 tsp Italian seasoning
- 1/2 tsp chopped red pepper
- 1/2 tsp sea salt
- 1/4 tsp black pepper
- 100 g grated Parmesan cheese

Cooking

- Arrange in a slow cooker: Italian sausages, bell peppers, onions, canned tomatoes, and minced garlic. Sprinkle with Italian seasoning, red pepper, sea salt, and pepper. Cook at low temperature for 6-8 hours.
- After cooking, put on plates and sprinkle with grated cheese.
- Serve with leafy greens, steamed broccoli or cauliflower rice.

201. Low carb goulash

Recipe

- 228 g shirataki noodles
- 0.5 tsp onion powder
- 2 minced garlic cloves
- 455 beef sausages or sausages
- 412 g diced tomatoes
- 25.25 g minced celery
- 1 pack of stevia
- 1 tsp salt
- 1 tsp chili powder

Cooking

- Drain the shirataki noodles, soak in water for 5 minutes, drain again, then fry in a dry pan, stirring constantly, until it starts to stick.
- Fry chopped sausage/sausages with onion powder and garlic until brown.
- Drain the fat as needed.
- Add the remaining ingredients.
- Stew for about 20 minutes, stirring often.

202. Low carb egg noodles

Ingredient

- 3 egg yolks
- 113.4 g soft cream cheese
- 0.13 tsp garlic powder fresh grated Parmesan cheese (about 1/3 cup plus 2 tablespoons)
- 37.33 g of freshly grated mozzarella cheese (about 1/3 cup plus 2 tablespoons)
- 0.13 tsp dried basil
- 0.13 tsp dried marjoram
- 0.13 tsp dried tarragon
- 0.13 tsp ground oregano
- 0.13 tsp ground black pepper

Cooking

- Beat egg yolks and cream cheese together. Add the parmesan and mozzarella, and continue whisking. Sprinkle with spices and beat well again.
- Put a baking sheet on parchment, and evenly distribute the cheese-egg mixture on it. Smooth with a spatula or the back of a spoon.

- Place the pan in the preheated oven to 246 ° C and reduce the temperature to 176 ° C.
- Bake 5 to 8 minutes. If small bubbles begin to appear, reduce the temperature to 148 ° C and continue to bake for 2-3 minutes until cooked.
- Let cool at room temperature for 10 to 15 minutes. Slice with a regular pizza knife or knife.

203. Baked ratatouille

Recipe

- 1 green zucchini
- 1 yellow zucchini
- 3 large tomatoes
- 1 eggplant
- 3 tbsp olive oil
- 1 tsp garlic powder
- 1/4 cup fresh basil
- 1 tsp salt
- 1 tsp black pepper
- 1 tsp oregano
- 1 cup low-carb tomato sauce
- Not necessary:
- 3 tbsp pesto
- 1/4 cup crumbled feta cheese

Cooking

- Thinly chop the vegetables.
- In a bowl, combine oil, garlic powder, oregano, salt, and black pepper.
- Put the chopped vegetables in a bowl of butter and seasonings, and mix.

- Put the tomato sauce on the bottom of the baking dish/dish.
- Lay the slices of vegetables on top, vertically in a circle.
- Place fresh basil between the slices.
- Cover the dish with foil and bake at a temperature of 170 degrees for 40 minutes.
- Remove the foil and make sure the vegetables are tender. Bake another 20 minutes without a lid.

204. Avocado roll with a vegetable salad

Recipe

- 55 g soft cream cheese
- 4 eggs, protein separated from yolks
- 150 g full whipped cream
- 200 g grated cheddar cheese
- 1/2 tsp salt
- 1/2 tsp black pepper
- 50 g grated Parmesan cheese

Filling

- Mashed 1 avocado
- 1 chopped cucumber
- 6 chopped cherry tomatoes
- 1/2 cup lettuce

Cooking

- Preheat the oven to 200 degrees.
- Beat cream cheese and egg yolk together.
- Add cream and mix.
- Add grated cheddar cheese and seasonings.
- In another bowl, beat the egg whites until foamy.
- Gently add the egg whites to the creamy mixture.
- Pour into a rectangular baking sheet with parchment.

- Sprinkle with half the cheese on top and bake for 12-15 minutes.
- Place a piece of parchment paper on the kitchen surface and sprinkle with the remaining parmesan cheese.
- Remove the roll from the oven, place it face down on parmesan-coated paper and let cool. Remove the top paper.
- Spread mashed avocado on a roll.
- Then sprinkle slices of cucumber, tomato, and lettuce.
- Roll up the roll, starting at one of the long edges, using the paper at the bottom.

205. Baked salmon with a nut crust

Recipe

- 4 salmon fillets
- 0.56 g walnuts
- 0.25 g grated parmesan
- 14.79 g lemon peel
- 4.93 g of olive oil

Cooking

- Preheat the oven to 200 degrees.
- Place salmon fillet on a greased baking tray (or lay it out with parchment paper).
- Grind the walnuts in the mill.
- Mix walnuts with parmesan, lemon and butter, and stir until paste forms.
- Put the walnut mixture on the salmon filet and press lightly to form a crust.
- Bake for 15 minutes.

206. Ginger Pumpkin Soup

Recipe

- 1 small pumpkin
- 44.36 g of olive oil
- 1 clove of garlic
- 1 small onion
- 0.5 l vegetable stock
- 7 g fresh ginger
- 2.46 g of salt
- 2.46 g black pepper

Cooking

- Cut the pumpkin in half and pull out the core.
- Trim the tail and pull out the seeds, and cut the pumpkin into cubes.
- In a large saucepan, heat 2 tbsp. olive oil.
- Add onions and garlic, and cook until tender, stirring frequently.
- Add pumpkin and ginger, and cook for 2-3 minutes.
- Add vegetable stock and bring to a boil.
- Season with salt and pepper.
- Cook over low heat for 35–40 minutes until the pumpkin is soft.
- Using a hand blender, beat the soup until smooth.
- Serve with whipped cream

207. Celery and Cauliflower Puree

Recipe

- 1 medium celery, peeled and diced
- 1 cup diced cauliflower
- 2 cloves of garlic, chopped
- 2 branches of thyme, chopped
- 1 tsp sea salt
- 2 tbsp avocado oil or olive oil
- ¼ cup coconut cream
- ¼ cup bone broth
- Black pepper to taste

Cooking

- Preheat the oven to 204 ° C.
- Mix chopped celery and cauliflower with garlic, thyme, salt, and avocado oil.
- Place on a baking sheet and cook for 35 minutes.
- Transfer to a blender or food processor, add cream and broth.
- Beat everything until mashed.

208. Braised cod in a tomato broth

Recipe

- 450 g wild cod fillet, chopped into small squares
- 800 g canned whole peeled tomatoes
- 1.5 cups chicken stock
- A small pinch of saffron
- 2 bay leaves
- 3 tbsp avocado oil
- Sea salt to taste

Cooking

- Add avocado oil to the pan over medium heat. Use your hands to squeeze the peeled tomatoes in a pan, then add the broth, saffron, bay leaf, and salt to taste.
- Bring the broth to a boil, then reduce the heat to a minimum.
- Add the cod fillet and cover, simmer for 5-7 minutes.
- Serve fish with tomato stock.

209. Benedict Salad with Bacon and Eggs

Recipe

- 3 strips of bacon
- 3 tbsp grated parmesan cheese
- 3 cups greens
- 6 halves of cherry tomatoes
- 2 medium egg yolks
- ¼ cup salted butter
- 1 tsp lemon juice
- 3 medium boiled eggs
- 1 tbsp dried green onions

Cooking

- Preheat the pan, and then fry the bacon on it until crisp. Drain the fat and cool the bacon.
- Lubricate the microwave oven oil pan. Put grated Parmesan cheese on it in the form of small "knolls".
- Microwave and bake the cheese until crisp. Allow cooling.
- Put egg yolks and lemon juice in a blender, and beat well.
- Melt the butter in the microwave until it begins to bubble. Add it to the previously beaten egg mixture and mix until the sauce thickens and becomes light in color.
- Put greens, chopped tomatoes and slices of bacon on a plate.
- Top with baked parmesan and boiled eggs.

- Pour the eggs with hollandaise sauce and garnish with onions.

210. Baked Eggs with Ham and Asparagus

Recipe

- 6 eggs
- 6 slices (about 100 g) Italian ham
- 226 g asparagus
- A few twigs of fresh marjoram
- 1 tbsp butter or ghee

Cooking

- Heat the oven to 176 degrees.
- Oil the baking tray with the muffin pan.
- Lay the ham down and around the hole so that it covers the bottom and sides.
- Add a few sprigs of marjoram.
- Pour 1 egg into each pan.
- Put in the oven and bake for 10 to 12 minutes until cooked.
- Pull out and allow to cool for several minutes.
- Steam the asparagus, then season it with oil.
- Put all the ingredients on a plate and enjoy.

211. Cabbage Keto Cutlets

Recipe

- 250 g finely chopped boiled cabbage
- 1 large egg
- 10 g coconut flour
- 29 g melted coconut oil
- Optional: salt and garlic powder

Cooking

- Put the cabbage, coconut flour, and extra seasonings in the food processor. Beat 3-4 times.
- Add the egg and butter, and beat 3-4 more times for complete mixing. Be careful not to chop the cabbage too finely. The mixture should be thick and sticky.
- Roll the cabbage mass into balls and form cutlets from them. You should have enough mix for 8 cutlets.
- Fry the patties until golden brown on both sides in a non-stick pan.
- Serve separately or with fat sour cream, fresh green onions or other herbs to your taste.

212. French pie with mushrooms, spinach and goat cheese

Recipe

- 6 large eggs
- 1/2 cup unsweetened milk to your taste
- 1 tsp thyme
- 1/2 tsp salt
- 1/4 tsp pepper
- 226 g chopped spinach
- 1 cup chopped mushrooms
- 1 large clove of garlic
- 56 g goat cheese
- 1 tbsp olive oil

Cooking

- Preheat the oven to 176°C. Beat the eggs, milk, thyme, 1/4 teaspoon of salt and a pinch of pepper in a blender. Set aside.
- Pour 1 tablespoon of olive oil into a large pot and place it on a small fire. Add mushrooms, garlic, and 1/4 teaspoon of salt and a pinch of pepper.
- Stew until mushrooms become soft (about 5-7 minutes).
- Lubricate the baking dish with butter. Put mushrooms and spinach with the first layer, then pour the egg mixture, and finally sprinkle with small pieces of cheese.

- Bake for 20-22 minutes or until the top is golden brown.
- Cut into six slices and serve.

213. Creamy cheese soup with vegetables

Recipe

- 2 cups broccoli (coarsely chopped)
- 1 medium carrot (chopped)
- 1 small onion (chopped)
- 2 tbsp olive oil
- 1 tsp garlic powder
- 3/4 tsp salt
- 1/2 tsp pepper
- 1/8 tsp nutmeg
- 2 cups chicken or beef broth
- 1 small spinach
- 1/2 cup fat cream
- 113 g Cheddar Cheese
- 113 g gouda cheese

Cooking

- Add olive oil to a large saucepan and put on medium heat. Add chopped carrots and onions, mix well and cook for 1-2 minutes. Add garlic, broccoli, seasoning, and spices. Mix and cook for another 1 minute.
- Add bone broth, mix and cook for 8-10 minutes until the vegetables are soft. Turn off the heat and mix with heavy cream.

- Pour 1/2 of the soup mixture into the blender, add the spinach and beat until smooth. You can mix the whole soup if you prefer a completely thick consistency.
- Return the contents of the blender to a large pan, and mix with two kinds of cheese until they are completely melted. Season to taste and sprinkle with broccoli and cheese if desired.

214. Creamy Spinach

Recipe

- 2 tbsp butter
- 2 tbsp olive oil
- 1 small onion, diced
- 2 minced garlic cloves
- 3 bunches of fresh spinach, about 425 g
- ¼ cup cream cheese
- 2 tsp salt
- 1 tsp pepper
- ¼ cup of fat cream

Cooking

- Heat the butter and olive oil in a skillet over medium-high heat.
- Add garlic and onions, and stir continuously for 2-3 minutes until soft.
- Add spinach (a handful at a time) and fry until it withers. Put in a thin strainer and squeeze out the liquid.
- Return the spinach to the pan, season with pepper and salt, and add the heavy cream. Cook until bubbles in cream.
- Mix with cream cheese until it is completely melted, and the mixture is thick and bubbly. Remove from heat and serve.

215. Cheese Halibut Cheese Bread

Recipe

- 450-900 g halibut (about 6 fillets)
- 1 slice of butter
- 3 tbsp grated parmesan
- 1 tbsp bread crumbs
- 1 tsp salt
- ½ tsp black pepper
- 2 tsp garlic powder
- 1 tbsp dried parsley

Cooking

- Preheat the oven to 204 degrees. Thoroughly mix all the ingredients in a bowl except platus.
- Dry the fish fillet with a paper towel and place each part on a baking sheet with parchment, oiled.
- Lay the cheese mixture into pieces of fish so that it covers its upper part.
- Bake the fish for 10-12 minutes (turn the pan at least once).
- Increase the heat by 2–3 minutes until the top is golden brown. Check for readiness with a fork.

216. Baked Eggplant with Cheese

Recipe

- 1 large eggplant, sliced
- A generous pinch of salt
- 1 large egg
- ½ cup grated Parmesan cheese
- ¼ cup pork greaves
- ½ tbsp Italian seasoning
- 1 cup low-sugar tomato sauce
- ½ cup chopped mozzarella
- 4 tbsp butter

Cooking

- Preheat the oven to 204 degrees. Place the chopped eggplant on a baking sheet laid out with a paper towel and sprinkle with salt on both sides. Let stand for at least 30 minutes to let all the water out of the eggplant.
- Combine minced pork greaves, parmesan and Italian seasoning in a shallow plate. Set aside.
- In a separate small plate, beat the egg.
- Melt the butter and grease the baking dish with it.

- Dip each piece of eggplant in a beaten egg, and then in a mixture of parmesan and cracklings, covering each side with crumbs.
- Place the eggplant in a baking dish and bake for 20 minutes. Turn eggplant slices over and bake for another 20 minutes or until golden.
- Top with tomato sauce and sprinkle with chopped mozzarella.
- Return the mold to the oven for another 5 minutes, or until the cheese has melted.

217. Shrimp with zucchini with alfredo sauce

Recipe

- 226 g peeled shrimp
- 2 tbsp butter
- 1/2 tsp chopped garlic
- 1/4 tsp chopped red pepper (optional)
- 1 tbsp freshly squeezed lemon juice
- 2 small zucchini
- 1/4 cup fat cream
- 1/3 cup parmesan
- Salt and pepper to taste

For garnish (optional)

- Chopped parsley
- 1 tsp parmesan cheese

Cooking

- Use a scoop to make noodles from zucchini.
- Heat the butter in a pan, add chopped garlic, red pepper and fry for 1 minute, stirring constantly.
- Add the shrimp and simmer for about 3 minutes. Add salt and pepper, remove from pan and set aside.

- In the same pan (with shrimp juice) add fat cream, lemon juice, parmesan, and cook for 2 minutes.
- Add the noodles from the zucchini and cook for another 2 minutes, stirring occasionally.
- Put the shrimp back in the pan and mix well.
- If necessary, add salt and pepper, garnish with parmesan and chopped parsley (optional) and serve immediately.

218. Keto mousaka with ground beef and zucchini

Recipe

For beef:

- 1 medium squash
- 280 g ground beef
- 3 tbsp low sugar marinara sauce
- 1 minced garlic
- 1/2 chopped onion
- 1 tsp dried oregano
- 1/4 tsp chili powder
- 1/2 tsp ground cinnamon
- 2 tbsp olive oil
- Salt and pepper to taste

For the sauce:

- 3 tbsp fat cream
- 3 tbsp cream cheese
- 85 g Gouda or Cheddar Cheese (chopped)
- 1 minced garlic
- Salt to taste

Cooking

- Cut the zucchini and put it on a baking sheet with foil. Drizzle with olive oil, sprinkle with salt and pepper and bake for 5 minutes or until golden brown.
- Heat olive oil in a pan, add chopped onion, chopped garlic and fry until soft. Add ground beef and seasonings, and sauté until tender. Add the marinara sauce, mix and cook for another 3 minutes.
- Combine half the crushed gouda or cheddar cheese, cream cheese, fat cream, garlic, and salt in a saucepan, and simmer until the cheese melts and the sauce becomes thick and smooth.
- Preheat the oven to 204 degrees. Put slices of baked zucchini on the bottom of the baking dish, put the beef mixture on top, pour the sauce and sprinkle with the remaining cheese. Bake for 20 minutes.
- Let the dish stand for about 5 minutes before serving. Serve with salad or greens.

219. Salmon fillet with vegetables

Recipe

Marinade:

- 56-113 g salmon fillet
- 2 tbsp fiber-free coconut or soy sauce
- 1 tbsp rice wine vinegar
- 1 tbsp avocado oil or olive oil
- 1 tsp sesame oil
- 2 tsp grated ginger
- 2 cloves of garlic (finely chopped)
- 1/2 tsp salt
- 1/4 tsp red pepper
- 1-2 tsp keto-friendly sweetener of your choice
- 4 cups roman salad

Salad:

- 2 cups of low-carb vegetables to your taste (cucumber, red cabbage, bell pepper, asparagus, spinach, bok choy, radish, etc.)

Cooking

- Put the marinade ingredients in a bag, add the salmon filet and let stand in the refrigerator for about 1 hour.
- Heat a large non-stick pan to medium-high heat. Fry the salmon on each side for 3-4 minutes until golden brown. Remove from heat and cool. If you want, cut it into small pieces. Also, the fillet can be baked in the oven (10-12 minutes at 204 degrees).
- Put salad, vegetables, and salmon in a bowl. Also add a side dish, sesame seeds, and herbs.

220. Salmon fillet with cream sauce

Recipe

- 2 tbsp olive oil
- 3 (170 g) salmon fillet
- 2 minced garlic cloves
- 1 cup oily whipped cream
- 28 g cream cheese
- 2 tbsp capers
- 1 tbsp lemon juice
- 2 tsp fresh dill
- 2 tbsp grated Parmesan cheese

Cooking

- Place a large frying pan over medium heat and heat the olive oil. Once the pan is hot, add the salmon fillet, sautéing each side for about five minutes.
- Once the salmon is cooked, remove it from the pan and set aside.
- In the same pan, simmer chopped garlic over medium heat until flavorful.
- Add heavy cream, cream cheese, lemon juice, and capers.
- Bring the mixture to a boil, stirring frequently to thicken.

- Once the sauce begins to thicken, put the salmon back in the pan and cover it with the creamy sauce.
- Reduce the heat to medium-low - just to heat the fillet.
- Garnish with fresh dill and grated Parmesan cheese.

221. Keto Blue Casserole

Recipe

- 226 g cooked chicken breast
- 226 g ham
- 113 g Gouda cheese
- 85 g cream cheese
- 1/8 cup grated parmesan
- 1/4 cup homemade mayonnaise
- 1/8 cup fat cream
- 1 clove of minced garlic
- 1/8 tsp black pepper
- 1/8 tsp nutmeg
- 3 slices of bacon (optional)

Cooking

- Heat the oven to 176 C. Dice the cheese and ham, chop the chicken, fry and chop the strips of bacon.
- Put homemade mayonnaise, fat cream and cream cheese in a bowl, then add grated parmesan, chopped garlic, seasonings and mix thoroughly.
- In the same bowl, put the chopped chicken, cheese and ham into cubes, and mix well.

- Put the resulting mass into a mold, sprinkle with chopped bacon and bake for about 25 minutes.

222. Salmon cutlets with parmesan

Recipe

- 170 g canned salmon
- ½ cup grated Parmesan cheese,
- ¾ cup fried pork skins (chopped)
- ½ cup mayonnaise
- 2 tbsp Dijon mustard
- 2 tbsp fresh lemon juice
- 2 tbsp fresh parsley
- 1 tbsp kajun seasoning
- 2 large eggs
- 2 tbsp olive oil

Cooking

- In a large bowl, mix canned salmon, half Parmesan cheese, half ground pork skins, mayonnaise, mustard, lemon juice, parsley and Khajun seasoning.
- Add the eggs and mix well.
- Form 4 cutlets of approximately the same shape and set aside.
- In a separate large bowl, combine the remaining Parmesan cheese and ground pork skins.
- Roll the patties in the previously obtained cheese mixture.
- Heat the olive oil in a large frying pan.

- Fry the cutlets in hot oil on both sides until crisp, about 5 minutes on each side.
- Remove from the pan and place on a paper towel to drain excess oil.

223. Jalapeno Cheese Pizza

Recipe

Dough

- 2 cups chopped mozzarella
- ¾ cup almond flour
- ½ tsp oregano
- ½ tsp paprika
- ½ tsp chopped chili peppers
- ½ tsp black pepper

Filling

- 1 tbsp tomato paste
- 1/3 slices of bacon
- 1/3 chopped jalapenos
- 11 tsp cream cheese
- ½ tsp garlic powder
- 3 tbsp chopped onion

Cooking

- Put mozzarella cheese in a microwave bowl. Add oregano, paprika, chili pepper, and black pepper. Jalapeno Cheese Pizza
- Heat the cheese in the microwave for about 1 minute or until it melts.
- Add almond flour to the cheese and mix until a dough is formed.
- Place the dough on a piece of parchment paper on a tray or in a pizza dish, and roll it out. Give it a round shape and curl the edges of the dough 2 inches toward the center of the pizza to make a crust.
- Spread the tomato paste on the dough.
- Using a teaspoon, place slices of cream cheese on top. Add jalapenos, bacon, onions and garlic powder.
- Bake at 176 ° C for 30-40 minutes.

224. Chile con carne

Recipe

- 450 g ground beef
- 450 g spicy Italian sausages
- 1 medium green pepper
- 1 medium yellow pepper
- 1 medium white onion
- 280 g canned jalapeno tomatoes
- 2 tablespoons curry powder
- 2 tablespoons chili powder
- 2 tablespoons of caraway seeds
- 1 tablespoon minced garlic
- 1 tablespoon coconut oil
- 1 tablespoon butter
- 1 teaspoon onion powder
- 1 teaspoon of salt
- 1 teaspoon black pepper

Cooking

- Take a large pan and place it on medium-high fire. Add butter and coconut oil, and let it melt.
- Add onions, peppers and chopped garlic. Heat the mixture, stirring constantly.
- Place the pan over medium heat, and add the hot sausage and minced meat.

- Fry everything until brown, adding salt and pepper to taste.
- Add onions, peppers, and garlic to the pot with beef and sausage.
- Add canned tomatoes, onion powder, and chili powder.
- Cook for about 20 minutes.
- Add curry powder and cumin, and cook for another 10 minutes, stirring frequently.
- Let it boil for 45 minutes to 2 hours, depending on which chili you want.

225. Keto Chili

Recipe

- 900 kg of young beef
- 226 g spinach
- 1 cup tomato sauce
- 1/4 cup Parmesan Cheese
- 2 medium green bell peppers
- 2/3 medium onions
- 1 tbsp. l olive oil
- 1 tbsp. l caraway seeds
- 1 1/2 tbsp. l chili powder
- 2 tsp cayenne pepper
- 1 tsp garlic powder
- Salt and pepper to taste

Cooking

- Chop onion and pepper. Then season with salt and pepper, and simmer in olive oil at medium-high heat, stirring occasionally. After the vegetables are ready, reduce the heat to a minimum.
- Fry the beef until brown. Season with salt, pepper and spices.
- Once the beef is fried, add the spinach. Cook for 2-3 minutes, then mix well.
- Add tomato sauce, mix well, then reduce heat to medium-low and cook for 10 minutes.
- Add the parmesan cheese and mix everything together. Then add the vegetables and mix again. Cook for a few minutes.

226. Rutabaga and Cauliflower Patties

Recipe

- 100 g rutabaga
- 100 g cauliflower
- 2 small shallots
- 4 tablespoons chopped beef
- 1 tablespoon chopped celery leaves
- 1 tablespoon chopped green onions
- ½ teaspoon white pepper
- ¼ teaspoon of salt
- 1 large egg
- 4 tablespoons of coconut oil

Cooking

- Cut the rutabaga into small pieces and fry in 1 tbsp. l coconut oil until brown.
- Grind rutabaga using a combine or blender.
- Put the cauliflower in the microwave and bring it to softness.
- Fry finely chopped shallots in 1 tbsp. l coconut oil until brown and crispy.
- Be careful not to burn it.

- Sauté the beef until brown, and season with salt and pepper.
- Add everything except eggs to the beef and mix well. Form small pies.
- Dip each pie in an egg (but not completely) and fry in batches in coconut oil until brown.

227. Spicy Sausage and Pepper Soup

Recipe

- 635 g spicy Italian sausages
- 6 cups raw spinach
- 1 medium green bell pepper
- 1 medium red bell pepper
- ½ medium onion
- 1 cup jalapeno tomatoes
- 2 cups beef
- 2 teaspoons chili powder
- 2 teaspoons of caraway seeds
- 2 teaspoons minced garlic
- 1 teaspoon Italian seasoning
- ½ teaspoon kosher salt

Cooking

- Cut the sausage and sauté it.
- Add chopped peppers, tomatoes, beef and spices to the pan. Add the sausage on top and mix well.
- Sauté your onions and garlic to a translucent state and add to the pan.
- Top with spinach and cook for 3 hours.
- After 3 hours, mix, reduce heat and simmer another 2 hours.

228. Ham and cheese pie

Recipe

- 340 g chopped cauliflower
- 2 cup chopped ham
- 1 ½ cup oily whipped cream
- ½ cup sour cream
- 2 ½ cup chopped hot cheddar cheese
- 1 cup diced mozzarella cheese
- ½ teaspoon black pepper
- ½ teaspoon garlic powder

Cooking

- Preheat the oven to 176 degrees.
- Put the cauliflower in a medium saucepan and fill with water.
- Bring cauliflower to a boil and cook for 8-10 minutes until cooked.
- Drain the cabbage, then grind it.
- Lubricate the 9 × 13 baking dishes and spread the mashed cabbage in it.
- Put the sliced ham on top of the cabbage.
- Combine the crushed cheese, sour cream, whipped cream and seasonings in a pan, and then cook over medium heat until the cheese is slightly melted.

- After evenly pour the mixture on top of the ham and cabbage.
- Put the diced mozzarella cheese on top of the casserole and bake for 40-45 minutes.

229. Shrimp and Cauliflower Curry

Recipe

- 680 g shrimp
- 5 cups raw spinach
- 4 cups chicken stock
- 1 medium onion
- 1/2 cauliflower
- 1 cup unsweetened coconut milk
- 1/4 cup butter
- 1/4 cup fat cream
- 3 tbsp. l olive oil
- 2 tbsp. l curry powder
- 1 tbsp. l coconut flour
- 1 tbsp. l caraway seeds
- 2 tsp garlic powder
- 1 tsp chili powder
- 1 tsp onion powder
- 1 tsp cayenne pepper
- 1 tsp paprika
- 1/2 tsp ginger (chopped, dried)
- 1/2 tsp coriander
- 1/2 tsp turmeric
- 1/2 tsp pepper

- 1/4 tsp cardamom
- 1/4 tsp cinnamon
- 1/4 tsp xanthan gum
- Salt and pepper to taste

Cooking

- Mix all the spices (except xanthan gum and coconut flour) and set aside.
- Cut 1 medium onion into rings.
- Heat in a pan 3 tbsp. l olive oil. Add the onion and fry it until soft.
- Add oil, 1/8 tsp. cream, xanthan gum, and spices. Mix well.
- After about 1-2 minutes, add 4 cups of chicken stock and 1 cup of coconut milk. Mix well and cover.
- Cook for 30 minutes. Divide the cauliflower into inflorescences and add it to the curry. Cook another 15 minutes.
- Peel the shrimp, add to the curry and cook for another 10-20 minutes with the lid covered.
- Add coconut flour and 1/8 tsp to the pan. xanthan gum and mix well. Cook for 5 minutes.
- After 5 minutes, add the spinach and mix thoroughly. Cook for 5-10 minutes with the lid closed.

230. Low Carb Chicken Stew

Recipe

- 450 g chicken
- 3 tablespoons peanut butter
- 4 tablespoons of soy sauce
- 1/3 yellow bell pepper
- 2 teaspoons sesame oil
- 2 stalks of green onions
- 1 tablespoon rice vinegar
- 2 teaspoons chili sauce
- 1/4 teaspoon paprika
- 1/4 teaspoon cayenne pepper
- 1 teaspoon minced garlic
- 1/2 lime juice
- 1 tablespoon of erythritis

Cooking

- Heat the sesame oil over medium heat, then add the chopped chicken and sauté it until brown.
- Then add all other ingredients. Stir well and continue cooking.
- After everything is ready, add the onion and 1/3 chopped yellow pepper.

231. Moroccan low-carb meatballs

Recipe

- Meatballs
- 460 g of young lamb
- 1 tbsp. l finely chopped fresh mint
- 1 tbsp. l finely chopped fresh cilantro
- 2 tsp fresh thyme
- 1 tsp chopped garlic
- 1 tsp ground coriander
- 1 tsp kosher salt
- 1 tsp ground caraway seeds
- 1/2 tsp onion powder
- 1/2 tsp carnations
- 1/4 tsp paprika
- 1/4 tsp oregano
- 1/4 tsp curry powder
- 1/4 tsp freshly ground black pepper

Sauce

- 1/2 cup coconut cream
- 2 tbsp. l coconut water
- 1 1/4 tsp caraway seeds
- 1 tbsp. l finely chopped fresh cilantro

- 1 tbsp. l finely chopped fresh mint
- Zest 1/2 lemon
- 1 tsp lemon juice
- 1/4 tsp salt

Cooking

- Preheat the oven to 176 ° C and mix all the meatball ingredients.
- Form 15-18 meatballs (or less if you want them to be large) and place them on the baking foil.
- Bake for 15-18 minutes or until the center of the balls turns pink.
- While preparing meatballs, mix all the ingredients for the sauce.

232. Casserole with bacon and cheese

Recipe

Meat filling

- 450 g of beef
- 1 tbsp. l fat bacon
- 2 tsp chopped garlic
- 1 tsp caraway seeds
- 1/2 tsp paprika
- 1/2 tsp chili powder
- 1/2 tsp salt
- 1/4 tsp cayenne pepper
- 1/4 tsp onion powder
- 1/4 tsp ground black pepper
- 1 tbsp. l low sugar ketchup
- 1 tbsp. l soy sauce
- 1 tsp fish sauce

Casserole

- 280 g bacon, chopped and fried
- 1 medium cauliflower, cut into inflorescences
- 113 g cream cheese
- 113 g cheddar cheese

Cooking

- Thoroughly mix all the ingredients for the meat filling (except for ketchup, soy and fish sauce). After mixing, put the mass in an airtight bag and add ketchup, fish and soy sauce.
- Lubricate the meat tightly inside the bag, seal it and place it in the refrigerator for at least 30 minutes.
- Cut the bacon into small pieces and fry them until crisp. Put on paper towels to cool.
- Add the beef mixture to the pan and sauté until brown. During this, chop the cauliflower into inflorescences.
- Place the inflorescences at the bottom of the baking dish and preheat the oven to 176 ° C. 6. Add ground beef and pieces of cream cheese.
- Finally, add the bacon and cheddar cheese, then pour the fat from the bacon on top.
- Bake for 40-50 minutes until the cheese is completely melted.

233. Stuffed Peppers Poblano

Recipe

- 450 g pork
- 1 tbsp fat bacon
- 4 peppers blanched
- 1/2 small onion
- 1 wine tomato
- 7 young champignons with brown hats
- 1/4 cup coriander
- 1 tsp caraway seeds
- 1 tsp chili powder
- Salt and pepper to taste

Cooking

- Bake peppers blanched in the oven for about 8-10 minutes. Turn them over every 1-2 minutes.
- Sauté the pork in bacon fat until brown - season with salt, pepper, caraway seeds, and chili.
- Add chopped onions and garlic. Mix everything together, then add the chopped mushrooms.
- Once the mushrooms absorb fat, add chopped cilantro and diced tomato. Cook another 1-2 minutes.
- Start the pepper with the resulting mixture and bake for 8 minutes at a temperature of 176 degrees.

234. Pepperoni Low Carb Pizza

Recipe

Pizza base

- 2 cups Mozzarella Cheese (~ 140 g).
- 3/4 cup almond flour
- 1 tbsp psyllium powder
- 3 tbsp cream cheese (~ 42 g).
- 1 large egg
- 1 tbsp Italian seasoning
- 1/2 tsp salt
- 1/2 tsp pepper

Filling

- 1 cup Mozzarella cheese (~ 113 g).
- 1/2 cup Rao tomato sauce
- 16 pieces of pepperoni

Cooking

- Microwave the mozzarella cheese until completely melted, then add all the other ingredients for the dough (except olive oil) and mix together.
- Knead the dough into a ball, then roll into a circle and grease the outside of the dough with olive oil.

- Bake the crust for 10 minutes at a temperature of 206 degrees. Remove from the oven, turn over and bake for another 2-4 minutes.
- Put the filling on top of the dough and bake another 3-5 minutes.
- Let cool slightly and serve!

235. Miso Salmon

Recipe

- 560 g salmon filet with skin
- Kosher salt to taste
- 3 tablespoons sake
- 2 tablespoons of white wine
- 3 tablespoons miso, best white

Cooking

- Cut the salmon into fillets. I had two large pieces, so I just cut them in half.
- Sprinkle the fillet with salt and let it lie down for 30 minutes. This will remove some of the moisture.
- Soak a paper towel with 1 tablespoon of sake and gently wipe the fillet with it.
- Mix 2 tablespoons of sake, 2 tablespoons of white wine and 3 tablespoons of miso.
- Pour about 1/3 of the marinade onto the bottom of the airtight container. Place the fillet in it, and then pour the remaining marinade on top. Cover and refrigerate for 1-2 days.
- When it is time to cook, preheat the oven to 204 ° C. Remove the marinade by scraping it off with your fingers.
- Use a piece of parchment paper on the baking sheet or grease the sheet well.

- 8. Bake salmon for 25 minutes.

236. Soup with red pepper and cauliflower

Recipe

- 2 red bell peppers
- 1/2 head of cauliflower
- 6 tbsp duck fat
- 3 medium green onions, diced
- 3 cups chicken stock
- 1/2 cup fat cream
- 1 tsp garlic powder
- 1 tsp dried thyme
- 1 tsp smoked paprika
- 1/4 tsp red pepper
- 113 g goat cheese
- Salt and pepper to taste

Cooking

- Cut the bell pepper in half and peel the seeds. Bake for 10-15 minutes or until the skin is charred and blackened.
- Once the pepper is ready, remove it from the oven and place it in a container with a lid or bag for storing food. Let the pepper steam to make it softer.
- Cut the cauliflower into inflorescences and season with 2 tbsp. molten duck fat, salt, and pepper. Bake cabbage for 30-35 minutes at 200 degrees.

- Remove the peel from the pepper by thoroughly cleaning it.
- Pour 4 tbsp into the pan. duck fat. When it heats, add the cubes of green onions, seasoning, chicken stock, red pepper, and cabbage. Cook for 10-20 minutes.
- Mix everything well with a blender, then add cream and mix again.
- Serve with crispy bacon and goat cheese. Garnish with thyme and green onions.

237. Jalapeno Keto Soup

Recipe

- 4 chicken thighs
- 1 tbsp chicken fat
- 3 diced jalapenos
- 2 tsp chopped garlic
- 1 tsp onion powder
- 1 tsp dried coriander
- 1 tsp seasoning cajun
- Salt and pepper to taste
- 3 cups chicken stock
- 170 g cream cheese
- 113 g cheddar cheese
- 4 slices of bacon

Cooking

- Preheat the oven to 200 degrees. Remove the bones from the thighs and bake the chicken for 50-55 minutes.
- Heat 1 tbsp. chicken fat in a saucepan over medium heat. Then add the chicken bones and cook for 5-10 minutes.
- Add diced jalapenos and minced garlic to the mixture. Cook 3-4 minutes or until soft.

- Add the broth and spices to the mixture and mix. Simmer until chicken thighs are cooked.
- Remove the skin from the hips. Remove chicken bones from the broth.
- Add extra chicken fat to the pan, and then use a blender to beat the jalapenos and garlic in the broth well. Grind the chicken and add it to the pan. Cook for 10-15 minutes.
- Add cream cheese and cheddar cheese to the soup, and mix, then boil for 5 minutes or until all the cheese has dissolved.
- Cook the chopped bacon at medium-high heat until crisp. Garnish the soup with it.

238. Salmon with cream sauce

Recipe

Fillet

- 450-550 g salmon fillet
- 3/4 1 tsp dried tarragon
- 3/4 1 tsp dried dill
- 1 tbsp duck, chicken or bacon fat, or ghee
- Salt and pepper to taste

Cream sauce

- 2 tbsp butter
- 1/4 cup fat cream
- 1/2 tsp dried tarragon
- 1/2 tsp dried dill
- Salt and pepper to taste

Cooking

- Cut the salmon in half to make 2 fillets. Grease the fish meat with spices and rub salt and pepper into it.
- Heat 1 tbsp. duck fat in a ceramic cast-iron skillet over medium heat. Then put the fillet skin down in it.
- Fry it for 4-6 minutes. Once the skin becomes crisp, reduce heat and turn salmon upside down.

- Cook salmon for about 7-15 minutes over low heat.
- Remove the meat from the pan and set it aside. Add oil and spices and brown. Then add the cream and mix well.

239. Keto casserole with tuna

Recipe

- 1 tablespoon butter
- ¼ cup chopped carrots
- ¼ cup chopped mushrooms
- ¼ cup chopped green onions
- 1 cup oily whipped cream
- ¼ teaspoon xanthan gum
- 226 g shirataki noodles
- ¾ cup chopped cheddar cheese
- 146 g of tuna
- Salt and pepper to taste
- Extras: almond flour

Cooking

- Melt the butter in a deep saucepan over medium heat.
- Add green onions, mushrooms and carrots.
- Stew vegetables for 3-5 minutes.
- Add xanthan gum over the vegetables.
- Add cream quickly and mix well.
- The mass will begin to thicken, but you continue to cook it until it starts to bubble.

- Place the shirataki noodles in the pan and pour in the prepared sauce.
- Mix with cheese and tuna.
- If desired, sprinkle with almond flour on top
- Bake at 175 ° C for 35 minutes.

240. Keto pizza in 5 minutes

Recipe

Pizza base

- 2 large eggs
- 2 tbsp parmesan cheese
- 1 tbsp psyllium powder
- 1/2 tsp Italian seasoning
- Salt to taste
- 2 tsp fat bacon

Filling

- 40 g mozzarella cheese
- 3 tbsp tomato sauce
- 1 tbsp fresh basil

Cooking

- Using a blender, mix all the ingredients for the base of the pizza in a bowl.
- Heat the oil in a pan until cooked, then pour the dough into it.
- After the edges are fried, turn the base over and cook for 30-60 seconds on the other side. Turn off the oven.
- Add tomato sauce and cheese, then bake for 1-2 minutes or until the cheese melts.

241. Bacon Keto Cheeseburger

Recipe

- 226 g ground beef
- 2 slices of pre-cooked bacon
- 28 g mozzarella cheese
- 56 g cheddar cheese
- 1 tsp salt
- 1/2 tsp pepper
- 1 tsp seasoning cajun
- 1 tbsp butter

Cooking

- Mix the ground beef with spices and make the patties with mozzarella inside.
- Heat 1 tbsp in a pan. oils. After it gets hot, put the patties in the pan.
- Cook them for 2-3 minutes, then put the cheddar on top, cover and continue to fry until cooked.
- Cut the bacon in half and place it on top of the hamburgers.

242. Pumpkin Keto Carbonara

Recipe

- 1 pack of Shirataki noodles
- 140 g Pancetta Bacon
- 2 large egg yolks
- 1/4 cup fat cream
- 1/3 cup Parmesan cheese
- 2 tbsp oils
- 3 tbsp Pumpkin Puree
- 1/2 tsp dried sage
- Salt and pepper to taste

Cooking

- Hold the shirataki noodles under hot water for 2-3 minutes. Pull it out and set it aside.
- Cut the bacon and place it in a hot pan. After the appearance of a crisp, remove from the pan, and leave the fat aside.
- Add oil to the pan and bring it to brown. Then mix with sage and pumpkin puree.
- Add fat cream and fat from the bacon to the sauce and mix well.
- Add shirataki noodles to the pan and cook for at least 5 minutes until a large amount of steam comes out of it.

- Add the parmesan cheese to the pumpkin sauce and mix well. Reduce the heat to a minimum and mix until the sauce thickens.
- Add the noodles and bacon to the sauce and mix well. Add 2 egg yolks to the sauce and mix.

243. Hot Chili Keto Soup

Recipe

- 1 teaspoon coriander seeds
- 2 tablespoons of olive oil
- 2 medium chopped chili peppers
- 2 cups chicken stock
- 2 cups of water
- 1 teaspoon of turmeric
- ½ teaspoon ground cumin
- 4 tablespoons tomato paste
- 450 g chicken thighs
- 2 tablespoons butter
- 1 medium avocado
- 56 g cream cheese
- 4 tablespoons chopped fresh cilantro
- Half lime juice
- Salt and pepper to taste

Cooking

- Cut and fry the chicken thighs in oil. Set them aside after cook
- Heat coriander seeds in 2 tbsp. olive oil to get more flavor and taste. Then add chopped chili to season the butter.

- Add broth and water, and let the mass boil. Mix with turmeric, ground caraway seeds, salt, and pepper.
- After boiling, add tomato paste and oil, and mix. Let it boil for 5-10 minutes.
- Add half lime juice.
- Place 450 g of chicken thighs in bowls and pour portions of soup. Serve each bowl 1/4 avocado, 15 g cream cheese, and cilantro.

244. Zucchini noodles with avocado cream and tomatoes

Ingredients

- 400 g zucchini
- 1 avocado
- 100 g Cherry tomatoes
- 10 g sesame
- 5 g olive oil
- 1 clove of garlic
- 2-3 stems basil
- 1 pinch each salt and pepper

Preparation

Preparation time: 10 minutes

1. Cut the zucchini into the pasta with a spiral cutter or peeler.
2. Peel a garlic clove and add it to the avocado along with the olive oil and some basil.
3. Puree the ingredients to a creamy mass.
4. Quarter the cherry tomatoes and put them under the avocado cream.
5. Season with salt and pepper and mix with the zucchini noodles.
6. Sprinkle with sesame and enjoy

TIP: If you do not tolerate raw zucchini so well, you can fry them briefly in a pan.

Nutritional values per serving

- Calories 450 kcal
- Carbohydrates 15 g
- Protein 10 g
- Fat 35 g

245. Vegan fitness kebab

Ingredients

- 1/2 packet   Vegan Döner (brand "Wheaty")
- 75 g   Parboiled Rice
- 2 tomatoes
- 1.2 onions
- 150 g   lettuce
- 150 g   Soy yogurt (brand "Alpro")
- Something   fresh herbs and spices
- Maybe something olive oil

Preparation

Preparation time: 20 minutes

1. Thoroughly wash the lettuce, tomatoes and onion and cut into small pieces
2. Meanwhile, cook the rice
3. Roast the vegan doner, he must be nice and crispy
4. Put the rice portion together with the salad, the tomatoes and the onions on a plate
5. Season the soy yogurt with fresh herbs and spices (maybe some olive oil) and pour over the salad
6. Finally, spread the fried vegan doner over it and season with some kebab seasoning

246. Gluten-free chickpea soup with Nutri-Plus Shape & Shake

Ingredients

1 Red onion

- 2 Garlic cloves
- 500 g   sweet potatoes
- 400 g   Chickpeas, cooked
- 1 cm   ginger
- 1 l vegetable stock
- 30 g   Nutri-Plus neutral protein powder, gluten-free
- About 1 tsp Salt, pepper, turmeric, nutmeg
- 1 teaspoon   coconut oil

Preparation

Preparation time: 20 minutes

1. First, free the onion, garlic and ginger from the shell, cut everything roughly and fry it in a little coconut oil.
2. Peel the sweet potato and cut it coarsely. Once the onions are glassy, you can put the sweet potato in the pot.
3. Stew everything together and then extinguish it with the vegetable broth.

4. Let it simmer for about 10-12 minutes until the sweet potato is tender enough, then add the chickpeas. Let everything simmer for another 5 minutes.
5. Get the soup off the stove. Then take a blender and puree the soup a bit.
6. Now add the protein powder and let the blender do the rest of the work. Mix the soup until no pieces are left. Season with the spices and enjoy.
7. If you like, then you can roast some chickpeas and add to the soup as a topping.

Nutritional values per serving

- Calories per serving 550 kcal
- Carbohydrates 90 g
- Fat 9 g
- Protein 38 g

247. Protein gnocchi with basil pesto

Ingredients

- 400g   Potatoes, boiling
- 60 g   Nutri-Plus protein powder, neutral
- 50 g   wheat flour
- 1/2 tsp   salt
- Something   nutmeg
- 2 tbsp Flour for the work surface
- 1 bunch   basil
- 30 g   pine nuts
- clove of garlic
- 100 ml   olive oil
- something   Salt pepper

preparation

Preparation time: 30 minutes plus cooling time

The recipe is actually a bit tricky. So take your time.

1. Peel potatoes, cut into small pieces and cook for 20-25 minutes.
2. Let the potatoes cool off !! (very important)

3. Put the pieces of potato, the protein powder, the flour and the spices together in a blender and mix everything together properly. The dough should have about the consistency of firm cake dough. If necessary, add flour or water.
4. Spread some flour on the work surface and divide the dough into four parts.
5. Moisten your hands to prevent the dough from sticking to your fingers and form long, round snakes out of the dough.
6. Slice the snakes every 1.5-2 cm, press briefly with a fork to keep the pesto better, and you're done with the raw gnocchi.
7. Now put the gnocchi together in lightly boiling water for 3-4 minutes and wait until they float up. Then they are done.

248. Vegan rosemary roulade with potatoes, broccoli and mushroom sauce

Ingredients

- 200 g   potatoes
- 200 g   broccoli
- 200 g   mushrooms
- 2 Rosemary-Vegan roulades (brand "Wheaty")
- 150 ml of plant milk
- 1.2onion
- 10 g   rye flour
- 1 tbsp   safflower oil
- Something   salt and pepper

Preparation

Preparation time: 20 minutes

Prepare the potatoes according to your preference (salt or jacket potatoes)

1. Meanwhile cook the broccoli in salted water for about 10 minutes
2. Clean the mushrooms and the onions, cut and fry in a pan for about 10 minutes over medium heat (in case of danger that the whole thing burns, please fill with a little water)

3. After the mushrooms and onions have softened, add the vegetable milk and bring to a boil. Simmer a little and bind with the flour, then season with salt and pepper.
4. Roast the rosemary and vegan roulades in a pan with a little oil on each side for about 2 minutes until golden brown
5. Serve on the plate and enjoy

249. Protein rice pudding

Ingredients

- 150-200 ml   Oatmeal or other vegetable milk
- 30 g   Nutri-Plus Shape & Shake Protein Powder Vanilla
- 2-3 tbsp   cooked rice
- Something   Cinnamon and Zucker light to sprinkle

Preparation

Preparation time: 7 minutes

1. Shake oat milk with protein powder in a shaker or blender.
- Mix with rice and warm in the microwave for a short time. But it also tastes cold.
- In the end, sprinkle with the cinnamon and sugar light mixture.

250. Vegan sliced à la Bombay

Ingredients

- 100 g   Vegan roast piece (brand "Wheaty")
- 75 g   Parboiled Rice
- 100 g   broccoli
- 150 g   pineapple

1.4   onion

- 100 ml of coconut milk
- Something   Curry, pepper and vegetable broth
- Maybe something Locust bean gum

Preparation

Preparation time: 25 minutes

1. Cook the rice
2. Chop the vegan roast and sauté
3. For the sauce, fry the onion and deglaze with coconut milk
4. Add the broccoli and cook
5. Season the sauce with curry, pepper and some vegetable stock (if the sauce is too liquid, you can use some carob seed flour)
6. In the end, add the pieces of pineapple (unsweetened) to the sauce

251. Summery bowls with fresh vegetables and protein quark

Ingredients

- 100g   green salad
- 100 g   radish
- 200g   kohlrabi
- 70g   carrots
- 70g   Red lenses
- 50g   tomatoes
- 2 spring onions
- 20g   Nuts / seeds
- 150 g   soy yogurt
- 2 tbsp mixed herbs
- 1 teaspoon   lemon juice
- 20 g   Nutri-Plus Shape & Shake, neutral
- 1 pinch salt, pepper

Preparation

Preparation time: 10 minutes

1. Wash the salad and the vegetables and peel the kohlrabi.
2. Simmer the red lentils for about 7 minutes.
3. In time, cut / grate the vegetables.

4. Mix the soy yogurt together with the lemon juice, the protein powder, some salt / pepper and the herbs.
5. Arrange all ingredients together in a deep plate or bowl and top with the spring onions and nuts / seeds.

252. Crispy asparagus tart with Nutri-Plus

Ingredients

- 150g   spelled flour
- 30g Nutri-Plus Shape & Shake Neutral
- 130ml water
- 8 g dry yeast
- 1/2 tsp salt
- 200g   soybean curd
- 2 tbsp mixed herbs
- 1 teaspoon   lemon juice
- 200 g   green asparagus
- 100 g   cherry tomatoes
- 1 Red onion
- 20 g pine nuts
- Smoothing Salt, pepper, chili flakes

Preparation

Preparation time: 30 minutes - plus walking time

1. Beginning with the dough!
2. Put the flour, our protein powder, the yeast and the salt in a bowl and mix all the dry ingredients thoroughly.

3. Second Now add the lukewarm water and knead everything together to a firm dough.
4. Leave the dough to rest for at least 30 minutes, taking care of the remaining ingredients over time.
5. Stir in the herb quark: Add the soy quark, the herbs, the lemon juice and some salt to a bowl and stir together.
6. Then wash the asparagus and the tomatoes and cut both small.
7. Peel the onion and cut into fine rings.
8. Put some flour on the work surface and roll out the dough as thin as possible.
9. Spread the herb quark on the flame cake batter and spread the remaining ingredients on it. Put the tarot cake in the preheated oven for about 10-12 minutes at 200 ° C. Finally, sprinkle the pine nuts on the tarot cake and taste it.

253. Protein-rich asparagus cream soup

Ingredients

- 1 kg   White asparagus
- 50 g   Alsan
- 40 g   spelled flour
- 1.2 l   water
- 200 ml of soy milk
- 30 g   Nutri-Plus protein powder neutral
- one pinch each   Salt, sugar, pepper, nutmeg
- 1.2 lemons
- Fresh parsley

Preparation

Preparation time: 45 minutes

1. You should wash the asparagus thoroughly and cut off the woody, dry ends.
2. Peel the asparagus and cook the skins in the water with a pinch of salt and a little sugar for about 20 minutes.
3. Drain the asparagus dishes and catch the asparagus water in an extra bowl.
4. Cut the asparagus into 2-3 cm pieces and cook them in the asparagus water for about 15 minutes soft.

5. Then pour the asparagus water with the asparagus pieces and let the Alsen melt in the pot. Once the Alsan has melted, add the flour and gradually add a little bit of asparagus water until the whole liquid is used up.
6. Now mix the soymilk with the protein powder and put the shake in the pot. Let the soup simmer a bit, but do not boil properly!
7. Now you can put the asparagus pieces, the lemon juice and the spices back into the soup and season to taste.
8. With fresh parsley serve and enjoy.

254. Meat and Kidney Pie

INGREDIENTS

- 500 g beef (diced)
- 225 g kidneys (cow or veal, heavy clean and cut)
- 1 onion (chopped)
- 150 g mushrooms (clean and sliced)
- 250 ml beef broth
- 2 tbsp. tomato paste (optional)
- 1 tbsp. cornstarch
- 250 g puff pastry (or broken dough)
- 1 egg (beaten)
- 1 tsp. salt
- 1 tsp. pepper (ground black pepper)
- 3 tbsp. oil
- water (to dissolve cornstarch)

INSTRUCTIONS

- Heat the oil in a casserole and brown the beef. We take it out and reserve it.
- In the same oil, we fry the onion until it softens.
- Add the kidneys, tomato paste, if used, mushrooms, and broth.

- Cover the casserole and lower the heat when the sauce begins to boil, letting it simmer until the meat is tender about 30 minutes.
- When it's almost done, we can start heating the oven at 180º C.
- Mix the cornstarch with a little water and add it to the casserole where the meat and kidneys are being cooked, mixing with the sauce, season with salt and pepper, letting the stew cook 5 more minutes, until the sauce thickens.
- We pass the meat and kidneys with their sauce to a baking dish.
- We stretch the dough enough to cover the source as a cover. We moisten the edge of the fountain with water and press the dough against the edge to seal it.
- We make a cut in the middle so that the steam can escape, and we paint the dough with a beaten egg.
- We put the meat and kidney pie in the oven and let it be done for 30 minutes, or until the dough that covers the cake is browned.
- We serve the cake very hot, almost as soon as it comes out of the oven so that the steam does not soften the dough.

255. Cauliflower and Pumpkin Casserole

INGREDIENTS

- 2 tbsp. olive oil
- 1/4 medium yellow onion, minced
- 6 cups chopped forage kale into small pieces (about 140 g)
- 1 little clove garlic, minced
- Salt and freshly ground black pepper
- 1/2 cup low sodium chicken broth
- 2 cups of 1.5 cm diced pumpkin (about 230 g)
- 2 cups of 1.5 cm diced zucchini (about 230 g)
- 2 tbsp. mayonnaise
- 3 cups frozen, thawed brown rice
- 1 cup grated Swiss cheese
- 1/3 cup grated Parmesan
- 1 cup panko flour
- 1 large beaten egg
- Cooking spray

PREPARATION

- Preheat oven to 200 ° C. Heats the oil in a large nonstick skillet over medium heat. Add onions and cook, occasionally stirring, until browned and tender (about 5 minutes). Add the cabbage, garlic, and 1/2 teaspoon salt and 1/2 teaspoon pepper and cook until the cabbage is light (about 2 minutes).

- Add the stock and continue to cook until the cabbage withers, and most of the stock evaporates (about 5 minutes). Add squash, zucchini, and 1/2 teaspoon salt and mix well. Continue cooking until the pumpkin begins to soften (about 8 minutes). Remove from heat and add mayonnaise.
- In a bowl, combine cooked vegetables, brown rice, cheese, 1/2 cup flour, and large egg and mix well. Spray a 2-liter casserole with cooking spray. Spread the mixture across the bottom of the pan and cover with the remaining flour, 1/4 teaspoon salt and a few pinches of pepper. Bake until the squash and zucchini are tender and the top golden and crispy (about 35 minutes). Serve hot.

256. Thai beef salad Tears of the Tiger

INGREDIENTS

- 800 g of beef tenderloin
- For the marinade :
- 2 tablespoons of soy sauce
- 1 tablespoon soup of honey
- 1 pinch of the pepper mill
- For the sauce :
- 1 small bunch of fresh coriander
- 1 small bouquet of mint
- 3 tablespoons soup of fish sauce
- lemon green
- 1 clove of garlic
- tablespoons soup of sugar palm (or brown sugar)
- 1 bird pepper or ten drops of Tabasco
- 1 small glass of raw Thai rice to make grilled rice powder
- 200 g of arugula or young shoots of salad

PREPARATION

- Cut the beef tenderloin into strips and put it in a container. Sprinkle with 2 tablespoons soy sauce, 1 tablespoon honey, and pepper. Although soak thoroughly and let marinate 1 hour at room temperature.

- Meanwhile, prepare the roasted rice powder. Pour a glass of Thai rice into an anti-adhesive pan. Dry color the rice, constantly stirring to avoid burning. When it has a lovely color, get rid of it on a plate and let it cool.
- When it has cooled, reduce it to powder by mixing it with the robot.
- Wash and finely chop mint and coriander. Put in a container and add lime juice, chopped garlic clove, 3 tablespoons Nuoc mam, 3 tablespoons brown sugar, 3 tablespoons water, 1 tablespoon sauce soy, and a dozen drops of Tabasco. Mix well and let stand the time that the sugar melts and the flavors mix.
- Place a bed of salad on a dish. Cook the beef strips put them on the salad. Sprinkle with the spoonful of sauce and roasted rice powder. To be served as is or with a Thai cooked white rice scented.

257. Stuffed apples with shrimp

INGREDIENTS

- 6 medium apples
- 1 lemon juice
- 2 tablespoons butter

Filling:

- 300 gr of shrimp
- 1 onion minced
- ½ cup chopped parsley
- 2 tbsp flour
- 1 can of cream/cream
- 100 gr of curd
- 1 tablespoon butter
- 1 tbsp pepper sauce
- Salt to taste

PREPARATION

1. Cut a cap from each apple, remove the seeds a little from the pulp on the sides, and put the pulp in the bottom, but leaving a cavity.

2. Pass a little lemon and some butter on the apples, bake them in the oven. Remove from oven, let cool and bring to freeze.
3. Prepare the shrimp sauce in a pan by mixing the butter with the flour, onion, parsley, and pepper sauce.
4. Then add the prawn shrimp to the sauce. When boiling, mix the cream cheese and sour cream.
5. Stuff each apple. Serve hot or cold, as you prefer.

258. A Quick Recipe of Grilled Chicken Salad with Oranges

INGREDIENTS:

- 75 ml (1/3 cup) orange juice
- 30 ml (2 tablespoons) lemon juice
- 45 ml (3 tablespoons) of extra virgin olive oil
- 15 ml (1 tablespoon) Dijon mustard
- 2 cloves of garlic, chopped
- 1 ml (1/4 teaspoon) salt, or as you like
- Freshly ground pepper to your taste
- 1 lb. (450 g) skinless chicken breast, trimmed
- 25 g (1/4 cup) pistachio or flaked almonds, toasted
- 600 g (8c / 5 oz) of mesclun, rinsed and dried
- 75 g (1/2 cup) minced red onion
- 2 medium oranges, peeled, quartered and sliced

PREPARATION:

- Place the orange juice, lemon juice, oil, mustard, garlic, salt, and pepper in a small bowl or jar with an airtight lid; whip or shake to mix. Reserve 75 milliliters (1/3 cup) of this salad vinaigrette and 45 milliliters (three tablespoons) for basting.

- Place the rest of the vinaigrette in a shallow glass dish or resealable plastic bag. Add the chicken and turn it over to coat. Cover or close and marinate in the refrigerator for at least 20 minutes or up to two hours.
- Preheat the barbecue over medium heat. Lightly oil the grill by rubbing it with a crumpled paper towel soaked in oil (use the tongs to hold the paper towel). Remove the chicken from the marinade and discard the marinade. Grill the chicken 10 to 15 centimeters (four to six inches) from the heat source, basting the cooked sides with the basting vinaigrette, until it is no longer pink in the center, and Instant-read thermometer inserted in the thickest part records 75 ° C (170 ° F), four to six minutes on each side. Transfer the chicken to a cutting board and let it rest for five minutes.
- Meanwhile, grill almonds (or pistachios) in a small, dry pan on medium-low heat, stirring constantly, until lightly browned, about two to three minutes. Transfer them to a bowl and let them cool.
- Place the salad and onion mixture in a large bowl. Mix with the vinaigrette reserved for the salad. Divide the salad into four plates. Slice chicken and spread on salads. Sprinkle orange slices on top and sprinkle with pistachios (or almonds).

259. Red Curry with Vegetable

INGREDIENTS

- 600 g sweet potatoes
- 200 g canned chickpeas
- 2 leek whites
- 2 tomatoes
- 100 g of spinach shoots
- 40 cl of coconut milk
- 1 jar of Greek yogurt
- 1 lime
- 3 cm fresh ginger
- 1 small bunch of coriander
- 1/2 red onion
- 2 cloves garlic
- 4 tbsp. red curry paste
- salt

PREPARATION

- Peel the sweet potatoes and cut them into pieces. Clean the leek whites and cut them into slices. Peel and seed the tomatoes.
- Mix the Greek yogurt with a drizzle of lime juice, chopped onion, salt, and half of the coriander leaves.

- In a frying pan, heat 15 cl of coconut milk until it reduces and forms a multitude of small bubbles. Brown curry paste with chopped ginger and garlic.
- Add vegetables, drained chickpeas, remaining coconut milk, and salt. Cook for 20 min covered, then 5 min without lid for the sauce to thicken.
- When serving, add spinach sprouts and remaining coriander. Serve with the yogurt sauce.

260. Baked Turkey Breast with Cranberry Sauce

INGREDIENTS

- 2 kilos of whole turkey breast
- 1 tablespoon olive oil
- 1/4 cup onion
- 2 cloves of garlic
- thyme
- poultry seasonings
- you saved
- coarse-grained salt
- 2 butter spoons
- 1/4 cup minced echallot
- 1/4 cup chopped onion
- 1 clove garlic
- 2 tablespoons flour
- 1 1/2 cups of blueberries
- 2 cups apple cider
- 2 tablespoons maple honey
- peppers

PREPARATION

- Grind in the blender ¼ cup onion, 2 garlic with herbs. Add 1 tablespoon of oil and spread the breast with this.

- Put in the baking tray, add a cup of citron and bake at 350 Fahrenheit (180 ° C) to have a thermometer record 165 Fahrenheit (75 ° C) inside, about an hour, add ½ cup of water if necessary.
- Bring the citron to a boil, add the blueberries, and leave a few minutes. In the butter (2 tablespoons), acitronar the onion (1/4 cup), echallot, and garlic (1 clove).
- Add the flour to the onion and echallot and leave a few minutes. Add the citron, cranberries, and honey and leave on low heat. Season with salt and pepper, let the blueberries are soft, go to the processor, and if you want to strain.
- Return to the fire and let it thicken slightly.
- Slice the thin turkey breast and serve with the blueberry sauce.

261. Parsnip soup, pear with smoked nuts

INGREDIENTS

For the soup:

500g of chopped parsnips, 1 tablespoon of olive oil, 4 sprigs of thyme, salt and pepper, 1 chopped onion, 1 tablespoon of margarine, 2 peeled and chopped pears, 800 ml of vegetable stock, 600 ml of milk, 75 g of crushed California Nuts until a flour texture is achieved

For smoked nuts:

2 tsp of maple syrup, 1 teaspoon of smoked paprika, 2 teaspoons of soy sauce, 50 g of California Nuts, 1 tablespoon of chopped scallions and a dash of olive oil to decorate

DIRECTION

- Preheat the oven to 180°C. Place the parsnips on a baking sheet and squirt olive oil. Season with thyme, pepper, and salt mix well and bake for 25-30 minutes until golden brown.
- Meanwhile, prepare smoked nuts. Mix the maple syrup, paprika, and soy sauce, spread on the nuts, and mix well. Position the nuts on a baking sheet and bake them for 8-10 minutes. Remove from the oven and let cool.
- Next, sauté the onion with the margarine over medium heat. Add the pear and continue skipping for 8-10 more minutes.

- Add the parsnip and the vegetable stock to the pan and continue cooking for 15 more minutes with the lid on. Add the milk and stir until creamy. Add the crushed nuts and season to taste.
- Place the soup in bowls and decorate with smoked nuts and chopped chives. Add a dash of olive oil and serve.

262. Moroccan style chickpea soup

INGREDIENTS

- 4 ripe tomatoes, chopped
- 250 g of cooked chickpeas.
- 1 chopped onion.
- 1 branch of chopped celery.
- 2 chicken thighs
- 2 tablespoons chopped fresh cilantro.
- 2 tablespoons chopped fresh parsley.
- 1 tablespoon turmeric.
- 1 tablespoon of cinnamon coffee
- 2 tablespoons grated fresh ginger coffee.
- A few strands of saffron.
- 4 tablespoons olive oil.
- A nip of sea salt and black pepper.
- Half grated zucchini with spiralizer (noodle substitute).

PREPARATION

- We marinate chicken thighs with cinnamon and turmeric.
- In a deep casserole, sauté chicken thighs in olive oil and brown them for about 3-4 minutes.
- Then add the chopped onion and grated ginger. We stir well.

- Add the celery, parsley, and cilantro. Saute the whole over medium heat for a few minutes.
- Next, we remove the chicken thighs and reserve them.
- Add the chopped tomatoes and a tablespoon of olive oil to the casserole.
- In a cup of hot water, we soak the saffron threads. Then add the saffron along with the water to the casserole.
- Then add the chicken and three more cups of hot water.
- Add the salt and pepper.
- Cover the casserole and let the whole cook for half an hour, stirring occasionally.
- Remove the chicken from the casserole, remove the bones, and add the shredded meat back to the casserole.
- Finally, we incorporate the chickpeas.
- Prepare the "spaghetti" zucchini with the spiralizer (noodle substitutes).
- We serve the soup in bowls, incorporating the zucchini spaghetti on top.

263. Tuscan soup of chard and white beans

INGREDIENTS

- 2 slices of finely chopped bacon
- 1 chopped onion
- 1 clove garlic minced
- 1/4 c. nutmeg (optional)
- 1/8 c. hot pepper flakes (optional)
- 6-7 cups chicken broth, or more as needed
- 1 can (540 ml) of white beans, drained and rinsed
- 2 tbsp. sun-dried tomatoes, chopped
- 1 piece of Parmesan rind (about 1/2 cup)
- 1 bunch of chard red or white
- 1/4 cup small pasta for soup
- 5 large sliced sage leaves
- 5 fresh basil leaves, chopped (optional)
- 1 C. grated Parmesan cheese, divided (optional)
- 1 C. extra virgin olive oil, divided (optional)

PREPARATION

1. In a big saucepan over medium heat, brown bacon with onion, garlic, nutmeg, and pepper flakes for 5 minutes. Add chicken broth and beans. Bring to a boil. Stir in the dried tomatoes and Parmesan rind. Reduce heat and cook for 10 minutes.

2. Meanwhile, seed Swiss chard and slice stems into 3/4 inch lengths. Cut the leaves into 1-inch wide strips. Add the stems and pasta to the soup. Reserve the leaves for later. Reduce to low heat and simmer gently until the pasta is tender about 10 minutes. Add Swiss chard and basil leaves and simmer for 3-4 minutes.
3. Transfer soup to bowls sprinkles with parmesan and drizzle with olive oil, if desired.

264. Blueberry jam, grapes, and chia seeds

What you will need

- 2 cups blueberries (previously frozen) thawed
- 1 cup red grapes
- 1 teaspoon lemon juice
- 3 tablespoons chia seeds
- Sweetener of your choice to your liking (optional)

Process

- Blend the grapes in a food processor until they are well chopped, but not completely like a porridge.
- Add the blueberries (including the juice that has melted), the lemon juice, and the chia seeds and blend, just to the point where everything is combined.
- Place the mixture in a jar or airtight container and refrigerate overnight.
- That's it! The jam stays fresh for a week.

265. Thick mushroom and wine sauce

What you will need

- 1 package (8 ounces or 225 gr) of cremini mushrooms
- 1 shallot
- 3 tablespoons brown rice flour
- ¼ cup of port wine (or any other wine)
- 2 cups of vegetable stock
- 2 cloves of garlic
- 1 teaspoon dried thyme

Process

- Preheat a wide skillet over high heat. No oil is needed. Cut the mushrooms and chop the shallot. Add them to the hot pan. Spread them in a single layer, sprinkle them with salt and let them brown. Cook until well browned, about 10 minutes.
- Add the brown rice flour and stir. Cook until the flour is no longer white and absorbs much of the juices.
- Make the sauce with what's in the pan and the port wine. Scrape any piece that has been left at the bottom of the pan. Add the vegetable stock, garlic, and thyme. Simmer with the pan partially covered, for at least 10 minutes.
- The sauce will be ready when it is thick.

266. Stuffed mushroom heads

What you will need

- 24 extra-large fresh mushrooms, or 40 medium-large mushrooms
- 2 cups chopped fresh spinach, well-drained
- 1 cup whole-grain wheat bread crumbs or gluten-free bread crumbs
- 1 large onion, finely chopped
- 5 minced garlic cloves
- ¼ cup of water
- 3 tablespoons low-sodium soy sauce (use wheat-free soy sauce if you are gluten sensitive)
- Salt or pepper to taste (optional)

Process

Preheat the oven to 350 ° F (177 ° C). Wash, cut the roots and set the mushrooms aside. Place the side of the stem on a non-stick baking sheet or lined with baking paper. Chop the mushroom's stems fine.

Heat the onion and garlic in a large casserole. Cook, stirring, for 2 minutes. Add the chopped stems of the mushroom and cook for 2 minutes more. Add spinach and soy sauce. Cook for another 2 minutes or so until the spinach wilts.

Add the crumbs of bread. Simmer until it absorbs all moisture. Salt and pepper season.

Place in each mushroom lid a small amount of the spinach mixture. Repeat until the whole thing is complete.

Bake, uncovered, for 15 to 20 minutes at 350 ° F (177 ° C).

267. Grilled Eggplant Sandwich

What you will need

- 1 medium eggplant (or 2 small zucchini)
- 1 to 2 tablespoons low-sodium soy sauce (use wheat-free soy sauce if you are gluten sensitive)
- 1 tablespoon balsamic vinegar
- 8 large, thick slices of whole-grain bread or gluten-free bread
- 1 roasted red pepper, sliced
- 1 large roasted garlic head
- 4 teaspoons of Dijon mustard (optional)
- 4 leaves of red lettuce

Process

- Cut the eggplant diagonally into slices 1/4 inch (6 mm).
- Brush the eggplant slices with soy sauce and roast them on a grill or iron skillet seasoned over medium-high heat for 2 to 4 minutes on each side until they are soft and lightly browned.
- Remove them from the pan and sprinkle with vinegar. Set them aside. Toast the bread, if desired and spread 2 to 4 cloves of garlic in the lower slice, add a layer of grilled eggplant, folding the soft pieces to fit in the slice of bread.
- Top with slices of roasted red pepper and lettuce. Spread mustard over the top slice of bread, if desired, then complete the sandwich and serve.

268. Creamy Cucumber Dip

What you will need

- 2 small cucumbers
- ¼ cup red onion, finely sliced
- 1 lb (453 g) firm tofu
- 3½ tablespoons lemon juice
- 2 peeled garlic cloves
- ¼ teaspoon coriander
- 1 pinch of cayenne pepper
- Salt or pepper to taste (optional)

Process

- Peel the cucumbers, remove the seeds, and grate them. Let them stand for 10 minutes.
- Combine tofu, lemon juice, garlic, salt, cilantro, cumin, and cayenne pepper in a blender. Combine them until the mixture is completely lump-free.
- Squeeze the cucumbers to remove excess moisture and then place them in a bowl with the red onion.
- Add the tofu mixture.
- Cool everything for 2 to 3 hours and serve.

269. Humus without oil

What you will need

- 3 cups cooked chickpeas (drained, but set aside the water)
- 6 tablespoons lemon juice
- 6 teaspoons minced garlic
- 3 to 4 teaspoons chili powder
- 1 teaspoon cumin
- 2½ teaspoons Dijon mustard
- Salt or pepper to taste (optional)
- Chickpea water, as needed

Process

- Mix all the ingredients well until you get a smooth and creamy consistency in a food processor.
- Add water from chickpeas, if necessary

270. Spiced carrot and white bean dip

What you will need

- ¼ cup vegetable broth without added salt
- 1 large carrot, grated
- 1 small brown onion, diced
- 1 crushed garlic clove
- 1 small red chili
- 1 teaspoon cumin
- ½ teaspoon of paprika
- ½ teaspoon ground coriander seed
- ¼ teaspoon of turmeric
- ¼ teaspoon cayenne pepper
- 1 cup cooked white beans (or a 15-ounce can (425 g), drained and rinsed)
- 2 tablespoons fresh lemon juice
- ¼ cup chopped fresh cilantro

Process

- Heat the vegetable stock in a small saucepan. Add the carrot, onion, garlic, and chili. Sauté over medium heat for 3 minutes. Add the spices and additional water needed to prevent the ingredients from sticking to the pan. Sauté the carrot and spice mixture for 5 minutes or until the carrots are soft. Remove from heat.

- Place white beans and lemon juice in a food processor. Add the spiced carrot mixture and mix until smooth.
- Transfer the mixture to a bowl and add the chopped cilantro. Refrigerate until cooled before serving.

271. Cucumber and kale open sandwich

What you will need

- 2 slices of whole-grain bread, toasted
- 2 to 3 tablespoons of hummus prepared without tahini or oil
- 1 chopped green onion
- ¼ cup chopped fresh cilantro
- 2 medium kale leaves, chopped into small bite-sized pieces (about the size of coriander leaves)
- ½ small cucumber
- Mustard of your choice
- Lemon pepper (Mrs. Dash and Frontier brands have no salt)

Process

- Spread hummus generously on toasted bread. Sprinkle the green onion, cilantro, and kale evenly over the hummus.
- Slice the cucumber in 8 circles and spread each with a thin layer of mustard.
- Place the cucumber slices, with the mustard down, on top of the coriander and kale layer and press down, if necessary, so that they remain in place.
- Sprinkle the open sandwich generously with lemon pepper, cut it in half or quarters, if desired, and serve.

272. Fried rice noodles with nut sauce and meatballs

Ingredients for 2 portions:

- 2 portions (handfuls) of rice noodles
- 1 packet of Dobra Kaloria meatballs or fried tofu / tempehu
- 2 tablespoons peanut butter
- 1 teaspoon chili paste or 1 fresh hot pepper
- 1 tablespoon coconut milk or 2 tablespoons soy drink
- juice of 1 lemon
- 2 carrots
- a small piece of leek (slightly green part)
- 1 clove of garlic a
- small piece of ginger
- favorite herbs (e.g., coriander, mint)
- optional: onion, zucchini, red pepper
- 1 teaspoon of rapeseed or sesame oil
- salt, pepper

process

- Pour rice noodles with warm water and let stand for about 30 minutes, soaked. You can also pour boiling water over it, but then it's enough to make it soft and sometimes overcooked.
- Grate garlic and ginger on small grater eyes and fry in a preheated oil pan. Add paste or chili and chop the carrot into

small sticks or peel with a julienne peeler. Chop the leek and additional vegetables and fry in a pan together with the carrots until tender.

- In a small glass, mix the peanut butter with milk/drink and add to the pan together with the rice noodles. Fry everything until it merges, and if necessary, add a little water.
- Throw the meatballs all the way until they just heat up. If you want them to be crispy on top, fry them in a separate pan and add only to the end to the pasta. Add herbs and season with pepper, salt, and lemon juice to the whole.

273. Spring pasta with sprouts

Ingredients for 2 portions:

- 2-3 handfuls of favorite wholegrain pasta (for me tagliatelle)
- 2 cups of frozen spinach
- 2-3 pieces of any vegetables: pepper, carrot, beetroot
- 1 handful of radish, broccoli or beet sprouts
- ½ cubes of natural tofu
- 1 tablespoon rapeseed oil
- 1 teaspoon smoked paprika powder
- salt, pepper

process

- Cook pasta with al dente according to the instructions in the package. Tofu crumbles in your hands and fry in a saucepan in oil, add smoked paprika.
- Dice the pepper, peel the carrot with a julienne peeler and grate the beet on a grater. Cut the sprouts from home-grown and rinse with water.
- Add vegetables to the tofu saucepan and lightly fry them, then add the spinach. When it is soft, add pasta, season with salt and pepper. Finally, add sprouts so as not to heat them and lose nutrients - spring noodles ready, tasty!

274. Mushroom tofu with smoked tofu

Ingredients for about 2-3 portions:

- 1 cube of smoked tofu
- 1 op. The Green Woodpecker Trill mushroom kaszotto or 2 cups of the home-made mixture
- 2 tablespoons olive oil and 1 tablespoon rapeseed oil
- 1 spring onion or chives
- about 2 ½ cup vegetable broth or water
- 1 teaspoon smoked paprika
- salt and pepper

process

- In a deep frying pan, fry the porridge with mushrooms in the olive oil until it sizzles, glazes, and smells beautiful. Then pour it ½ cup broth or water and bring to a boil. Stirring the groats every now and then, add the rest of the broth and, if necessary, water until the groats are soft. Season to taste with paprika, salt, and pepper.
- Tofu cut into cubes and fry in hot oil until browned. Add chopped onion and fry for a while.
- Transfer the finished cassotto to a deep plate, put tofu on it and sprinkle with chopped chives.

275. Asian tofu with soba noodles

Ingredients for 2 servings:

- 2 servings of soba noodles
- 1 cube (180 g) of natural or smoked tofu
- 1 small white onion
- 1 spring onion
- 1 clove of garlic
- 1 medium carrot
- 2 cups of small broccoli florets
- ¼ cup of soy sauce
- 2 teaspoons brown sugar
- ⅓ cup of water
- 3 tablespoons oil
- salt, pepper to taste

process

- Tofu cut into narrow sticks and fry in a pan in hot oil until golden and crispy on both sides - preferably do not move it, just wait patiently and watch it sizzle. Put the finished tofu into a bowl and take care of the sauce.
- Fry chopped garlic and onions in the same pan you used to prepare tofu. Add soy sauce, brown sugar, and water. Bring to a boil, then reduce the heat and allow excess liquid to evaporate slowly. The sauce should be slightly reduced.

- In the meantime, cook the pasta.
- Put the fried tofu on the pan with the sauce and mix thoroughly so that the whole is covered with the sauce. Add to it tiny florets of broccoli and carrots grated on coarse mesh or mandolin.
- Transfer the pasta to the lunchbox, pour the sauce from the pan into a separate container, and take it all with you to work.

276. Marinated portobello steaks

Ingredients for about 5 mushrooms:

- 3 tablespoons balsamic vinegar
- 2 tablespoons soy sauce
- 2 tablespoons maple syrup
- 1 teaspoon mustard
- 2 cloves garlic
- 1 chili pepper
- salt, pepper
- 5 portobello mushrooms or a dozen ordinary mushrooms
- favorite vegetables to serve
- oil for frying

process

- Peel the garlic and cut the chili pepper into smaller pieces, and optionally remove the seeds from it (if you don't like spicy foods). Mix all marinade ingredients thoroughly with a blender or knead in a mortar.
- Wash portobello mushrooms and cut off their stems. In a large bowl, rub them well with the marinade (preferably with gloved hands) and set aside for a minimum of 15 minutes, preferably a few hours (you can prepare the whole day the day before and fry the next day).

- Fry marinated mushrooms in a grill pan or ordinary pan pressing the mushrooms until they are all soft. You can also arrange them on the grill or even over the fire.
- Serve ready mushrooms with your favorite vegetables, pour the rest of the marinade and eat with a crispy baguette.

277. Chickpeas meatballs - like from a Swedish buffet

Ingredients

- 1 cup chickpea flour
- 1 red pepper
- 1 cup canned corn (in the season from the cob, out of season from the jar)
- 1 cup of frozen green peas
- 1 teaspoon curry spice
- 2 tablespoons yeast flakes (optional)
- 2 tablespoons soy sauce
- 2 tablespoons canola oil
- water
- salt, pepper

process

- Sieve chickpea flour through a sieve into a large bowl, add spices and mix. Cut the peppers into small cubes, pour the sweetcorn and peas with warm water.
- Add ½ cup of lukewarm water and all vegetables, soy sauce, and oil to the bowl. Mix the ingredients together and add more water if necessary until an adhesive mass forms. Stand for several minutes.

- The mass for meatballs should be thick, but it must not be too dry - it can be easily formed. Form balls with wet hands and place them on a baking tray lined with baking paper.
- Place the meatballs in the oven preheated to 190 ° C and baked for about 30 minutes until crispy and browned.

278. Caldo Verde - Portuguese kale soup

Ingredients

- ½ kg of potatoes or just a few medium pieces of
- about 2-3 handfuls of chopped kale (without thick stalks)
- less than 1 liter of vegetable broth
- 1 white onion
- 1 clove of garlic
- 1 tablespoon of olive oil
- 1-2 tsp smoked peppers (for soup and serving)
- salt, pepper
- toppings: smoked tempeh, fried tofu, crispy baguette (optional)

Process

- Fry finely chopped onion in olive oil and grated garlic on a grater.
- Add the previously peeled and diced potatoes and fry for about 10 minutes together with the onion.
- Then pour the whole broth and cook until the potatoes are soft.
- Pull out half the potatoes one after the other and set aside in a bowl for a while, and mix the soup in a pot with a hand blender. Then add the rest of the potatoes and chopped kale

pieces. Cook for a few minutes until the kale softens and has a light green color.
- Season the soup with generous pepper and salt and smoked paprika.
- Serve with fried tempeh or tofu and eat with a crispy roll.

279. Tomato cream of red lentils

Components

- ¾ cup dry red lentils
- 1-2 canned tomatoes pelati (in season 2-4 cups of sliced fresh)
- 1 white onion
- 1 clove of garlic
- 1 large carrot
- 1 tablespoon oil rapeseed
- 1-2 tablespoons of juice of a lemon
- 1-2 teaspoon cumin (cumin)
- 1 teaspoon smoked pepper (preferably acute)
- 1 teaspoon savory or lovage
- teaspoon thyme
- decoction vegetable or water
- salt, pepper
- to serve: buckwheat, parsley, coriander

Process

- In a thick-bottomed pot or deep saucepan, heat the oil and fry the finely chopped onion, then add garlic.
- Then add the diced carrot and the washed lentils and pour the vegetable stock so that it fully covers all ingredients to a height of 2-3 cm. Cook until carrots and lentils are soft.

- When the vegetables soften, add canned tomatoes and spices. Boil for another 10-15 minutes, then blend with a hand blender, add lemon juice and season to taste. Serve with buckwheat and fresh herbs.

280. Simple miso soup - for a cold!

Instead of the classic chicken broth, you can choose a vegetable decoction full of rich aromas. However, when a cold catches us, who wants to stand a few hours over the boiling broth? The miso soup is coming to the rescue, ready in 10 minutes - and even less!

Ingredients

- 500 ml of water or vegan dashi broth
- 2 - 3 tablespoons light miso paste
- half a bunch of onions spring onions
- 100 grams of natural tofu or more
- 1 sheet of nori
- Pak Choy algae , any green leafy vegetable, even our good kale
- soy sauce (optional)

Process

- Boil water in a medium saucepan and add chopped burrow algae into small rectangles. Boil and keep on very low or even off the fire. Add miso paste and mix thoroughly. You can mix it in a small amount of water and only then add to the entire saucepan - there will be no lumps.
- Dice the tofu, chop the spring onions and green park choy / kale leaves and add them to the hot soup. Instead of salt

(although the paste itself is quite salty already), add soy sauce to the soup - if you feel the need.
- Hold the stove for a while, and it's ready! Serve in small bowls with extra spring onions

281. Warming cream of baked vegetables

Thick and aromatic soup-cream is the best way to warm up during cooler summer-autumn evenings. You will prepare this cream in 30 minutes, and it will warm you up for long hours.

Ingredients

- 3 smaller carrots
- half of the medium celery root
- 1 sweet potato
- 1 medium plain potato
- 1 medium white onion
- 4 cloves of garlic
- 1 teaspoon grated fresh ginger
- 3 teaspoons tomato paste
- 2 tablespoons olive oil
- ½ liter - 1-liter vegetable broth fungal or
- 1 teaspoon pepper smoked, e.g., the
- 1 teaspoon of hot pepper, for example. the
- half teaspoon cumin
- salt and pepper
- to give: toasts, cream Sunflower

Process

- Scrub the sweet potato, carrot, potato, and celery thoroughly, peel only the celery. Cut them all into 2 cm cubes and put them

in a wide bowl. Add tomato paste and rub all the vegetables with it, it's best done with your hands.
- Heat the oven to 190 degrees, line the baking tray with baking paper and spread the vegetables on it along with the peeled garlic. Bake until all the vegetables are soft and remove the garlic earlier, after about 15 minutes, so that it does not burn and is not bitter.
- In the meantime, fry the chopped onion in the frying pan with olive oil until it is vitrified. Add the grated ginger now and choke everything for a moment, stirring vigorously.
- Put the roasted vegetables into a pot or a blender and add onion and ginger. Mix at low speed, adding a little broth until you get the consistency you want. Add spices and season with salt and pepper.
- Serve with warm croutons, a blend of sunflower cream, and your favorite sprouts.

282. Watermelon gazpacho in a jar

The world's best summer cold soup made from fresh and aromatic tomatoes. It encourages you to try its cooling taste, but also the simplicity of preparation.

Ingredients

- 1kg of ripe, aromatic tomatoes (I use a buffalo heart)
- half a red pepper +
- half a small chili pepper
- 3 ground cucumbers
- 1 onion
- 1 clove of garlic (optional)
- 2 cups cubed watermelon
- juice of 1 lemon
- a handful of leaves basil
- a handful of mint leaves
- 1 - 2 tablespoons olive oil
- salt, pepper

Process

- Tomato peel slightly cut in several places, then transfer the tomatoes to a deep pot and pour boiling water, let stand for a few minutes. Drain the water and peel the tomatoes from the skin, but this is not a necessary stage if the skin does not bother you.

- Peeled tomatoes in half and put in a blender cup or larger bowl. Add chopped onion, garlic, diced peppers, cucumbers, chili peppers, and lemon juice. Also, add basil and mint leaves. All mix well in a blender or using a hand blender, finally adding olive oil.
- Then add chopped pieces of watermelon and mix only for a moment, so that the remaining watermelon particles can be felt. Season with salt and pepper to taste.
- Serve well chilled with diced paprika, lemon juice, stale bread, and a large dose of fresh, chopped basil.

283. Mango soup with cider and chili

This cooler is an offer for those who want to cool off in the raging heat, but also want something sweet and spicy. Mango and chili are the best combination and ready in less than 10 minutes.

Ingredients

- 3 large pieces of ripe, soft mango
- approx. 150 ml of cider or mineral water
- 1 medium chili pepper
- 3 pinches of cardamom
- 1 tablespoon of coconut milk or soy cream (optional, but I recommend)
- fresh mint leaves

Process

- Peel the mango by removing pieces from the stone and then separating the flesh from the skin. Transfer them to a hand blender, cup blender, or one with "S" knives.
- Add a little water or cider; mix everything into a smooth cream, gradually adding the liquid until you get the consistency you want. Then add a little coconut milk or vegan cream.
- Pour the cooler into an airtight container or jar and cool to a low temperature, before serving you can even keep it in the freezer for a while.

- Serve the cooler in a bowl and add chopped chili on top of the liquid (remember to wash your hands and all tools that have come into contact with the chili) and fresh mint. Stir everything before eating.

284. Peanut sweet potato ginger cream

Ideal when it comes to creams. Warming, filling, and easy to prepare. With the addition of pinching ginger and peanut butter.

Ingredients

- 1 larger sweet potato (about 400 - 500g)
- 1 leek (white and light green part)
- 1 carrot
- 1 clove of garlic a
- bit of olive oil
- 2 - 3 tablespoons of peanut butter (the best will be without salt)
- 2cm fresh ginger, grated on a grater
- 1.5l vegetable broth a
- few pinches of pepper (hot or fresh)
- salt, pepper

Process

- Peel the garlic and chop it with the leek, then fry in a large pot on the hot oil until the leek is soft.
- Add diced sweet potato and carrot (I do not peel, I scrub properly). Add a little salt and pepper, stew for a few minutes.

- Pour over the vegetable broth and cook on medium heat until sweet potato and carrot are soft.
- When the vegetables are ready, add the ginger and mix it into a smooth cream.
- Then add the peanut butter before mixing it in a small bowl with a little cream - so that the butter mixes well. Season to taste with salt and pepper and paprika. Eat with croutons (e.g., baked) tofu, sprouts, or good bread, tasty!

285. Pumpkin spice syrup

Spicy, warming - for the iconic coffee, porridge, but also for ice cream and desserts. Pumpkin spice syrup is a must in the autumn kitchen!

Ingredients

- ¾ cup thick coconut milk
- 1 cup pumpkin purée
- ¾ cup brown sugar
- ½ cup soy or almond milk 1 mig
- teaspoon ground cinnamon
- ½ teaspoon ground vanilla (or 1 teaspoon vanilla extract)
- 1 teaspoon anise grains
- pinch of salt

Process

- Heat coconut milk in a saucepan, add sugar, pumpkin puree (baked and mixed pumpkin), and all spices. If you use very thick mashed potatoes, add some soy milk to get a smooth consistency. 2. Hold it for several minutes on low heat until the sugar dissolves and the liquid thickens a Little. Season again to taste, without forgetting the salt, which conquers all other spices by itself. 3. Pour the syrup through a sieve into a medium bottle, and when it cools down, close it tightly. You can store it in the fridge for several weeks.

286. Matcha vegan cheesecake

A classic cashew cheesecake, but extremely creamy and mild, with a hint of Japanese matcha tea flavor. It is simple to make because you only need a blender and a moment in the kitchen. Matcha vegan cheesecake is the perfect dessert for white wine and gossip with friends, but also for a date!

Ingredients

- 2-3 teaspoons matcha tea
- ½ cup maple syrup (or agave)
- ¼ cup of coconut oil
- juice from 1 lemon a
- bit of vanilla extract a
- pinch of salt a
- few spoons of pistachios

Process

- Prepare your favorite cheesecake bottom and transfer it to a sheet covered with cling film.
- Soak cashews in water - preferably all night or 2-3 hours in boiling water. Transfer them to a blender together with syrup, oil, extract, and salt. Mix everything to a smooth mass, the longer - the consistency will be creamier. At the end of mixing, add lemon juice, controlling the sour taste of the mass - I like it when the mass is quite acidic, but you can overdo it.

- Put just over half the weight into the previously prepared mold on the bottom. Add the matcha tea gradually to the remaining mass, mixing all the time until all the lumps disappear. Every now and then, check if the tea is already palatable so as not to overdose it - the mass may come out too bitter.
- Tap the cheesecake tray on the kitchen counter to get rid of air from the mass. Sprinkle the top of the cheesecake with chopped pistachios and transfer to the freezer. The cheesecake will be ready after a few hours, and before eating, pull it out about 30 minutes before serving.

287. Vegan delicacies

Iconic cakes with jelly and chocolate coating - but in a fully vegetable version. Vegan delicacies are great sweets that you can easily prepare yourself at home.

Ingredients

- **sponge cake:** 1 cup
- incomplete wheat flour ⅔ cup sugar
- ½ cup of soy milk
- 3 tablespoons neutral oil (rapeseed, grape seed, coconut) a bit of vanilla extract (optional)
- ¼ teaspoon baking powder
- pinch of salt
- 1 vegan pack * orange jelly or another favorite
- **topping:** 1 bar of dark chocolate
- 3-4 tablespoons of soy milk
- 1 small teaspoon of coconut oil (optional)

Process

- .Mix all the dry biscuit ingredients in a larger bowl and add soy milk and oil to them. Mix them well until a dough forms.
- Cover the muffin mold with baking paper or grease with a little oil and pour it into each cavity the right amount of dough (so that there are enough for about 10 cakes).
- Bake in an oven preheated to 180 ° C for about 8-10 minutes. Then cool and remove the ready biscuits from the molds.

- Make the jelly from the recipe given on the package, which you then put in to cool and cool in the fridge.
- To prepare the coating, dissolve the chocolate in a water bath and add soy milk and a little oil to it.
- Put 1 tablespoon of ready jelly on the biscuits prepared earlier and dipped or pour the prepared topping. Set the cakes to cool, then make sure they do not disappear too quickly.

288. Christmas cocktail - vegan eggnog

Traditional American Christmas cocktail - vegan eggnog with the addition of aromatic brandy or whiskey. In my plant version based on cashews, dates, and spices. Perfect for joint feasting at the table with the family!

Ingredients

- 1 cup cashew nuts
- 1 cup soy or almond milk
- 2-3 glasses of water
- about 5 pieces of dates (more if you like sweeter drinks)
- 2-3 scoops of brandy or whiskey
- 1 tablespoon lemon juice (optional, to taste)
- 1-2 teaspoons cinnamon
- ½ teaspoons ground anise
- ½ teaspoons ground ginger
- 2 pinches nutmeg
- pinch of salt

Process

- Pour dates and cashews with boiling water and leave to soak for 20 minutes. Transfer the remaining ingredients to the blender dish and finally add the drained nuts and dates.
- Mix thoroughly in a high-speed blender for a few minutes, until a thick and creamy cocktail without lumps is formed. If

your blender can't do it, mix the cashews with water first and strain them with gauze.
- Season the cocktail with more lemon juice and salt to taste, and if you prefer sweeter drinks, add 2-3 pieces of dates. Serve it chilled with a pinch of cinnamon.

VEGETABLE RECIPES

327. Boar stew with vegetables, herbs and plums, a Tuscan recipe

Ingredients

- 1 kg   Wild boar from the club without fat and bone
- 1 Onion
- 2 pole / s celery
- 1 Carrot
- 5 Juniper berry
- 1 Garlic cloves)
- 1 branch / s   rosemary
- 1 branch / s   Marjoram or dried rubbed
- 1 branch / s   thyme
- 3 / 4 liters   Red wine, (Chianti)
- 60 ml   Vinegar, (red wine vinegar)
- 3 tbsp   Flour
- 30 g   pine nuts
- some   Prune
- 30 g   Chocolate, bitter, grated
- 6 tbsp   olive oil
- salt
- Aceto balsamico

Preparation

1. Cut the wild boar meat into cubes of about the same size and place it in a bowl. Add the wine, the sliced onion, celery and carrot bits, crumbled bay leaf, crushed juniper berries, marjoram, thyme, crushed garlic and rosemary. Cover with the marinade and let it simmer for 24 hours, stirring several times.
2. Remove the pieces of meat, drain, dab and turn in the flour. Remove vegetables and herbs with a slotted spoon from the marinade and set aside.
3. Heat the oil in a saucepan and sauté the vegetables and herbs from the marinade. Take out and sear the meat well in the hot fat from all sides. Add the vegetables and herbs and deglaze with the marinade. Cover and stew for about 3 hours on the lowest heat setting.
4. After 1 ½ hour, remove the meat with a slotted spoon and place on a plate. Fish the herb sprigs from the sauce and purée the gravy carefully with a wand. Put the meat and sauce back in the pot. Add the finely chopped pine nuts, the prunes cut into fine strips and the dark chocolate. Pour in the red wine vinegar and stew for another 1 ½ hours. Season with some balsamic vinegar and salt.

328. Turkish ACMA with sheep's cheese and vegetables

Ingredients

For the dough:

- 100 ml of water
- 100 ml of milk
- 100 ml of oil
- 200 g   Quark
- 1 tbsp   salt
- 3 tbsp   sugar
- 2 pck.   Yeast, fresh
- 100 ml cream
- 700 g   Flour
- 1 pck.   baking powder

For the filling:

- 200 g   feta cheese
- 1/2 Bund   parsley
- For the decoration:
- 10 Cherry tomato
- 2 pepperoni
- 10 olives

Preparation

1. For the dough, mix all the liquid ingredients together. Mix the flour and baking powder together, add gradually and prepare the dough. Leave the dough in a warm place for 45 minutes.
2. Form small balls from the dough, brushing the hands with oil. Layout a baking tray with baking paper and place the balls over it. Cover your hands with oil every now and then. Make a recess with your fingers in the balls and fill them with sheep's cheese and parsley. Decorate with tomatoes, peppers and olives and let the balls go for another 15 minutes.
3. Brush with egg yolks and bake in a preheated oven at 160 ° C for 20 - 25 minutes.

329. My creamy, vegan peanut fritters with vegetables and soy

Ingredients

- 3 / 4 cup soya granules
- n. B. Vegetable broth, hot, for soaking
- 1 m. -Large Onion (s), diced
- 1 Garlic clove (s), crushed
- 1 / 2 m.-large Carrot (s), diced
- 1 / 2 m.-large Zucchini, diced
- 1 can Corn, (or 140g vegetable corn)
- 100 ml Vegetable stock, strong
- 150 ml of Soy milk (soy drink)
- 3 tbsp soy sauce
- 3 tbsp peanut butter
- 1 tbsp parsley
- Something chili powder
- Something pepper
- Possibly. curry powder
- Possibly. paprika
- Something Vegetable oil, for searing
- Possibly. Flour, to thicken

Preparation

1. Soy granules in a bowl. Bring the vegetable stock to a boil and pour over the granules. It should not be in the "dry" and swell well. Let it swell for at least 5 minutes. Then express properly and possibly season with a little salt or broth (can taste nice strong).
2. Heat vegetable oil in the pan and add the granules. The best taste is achieved in my opinion, if you let the granules neatly burn until it is really nice browned and crispy.
3. Then add the diced onions, carrots and the crushed garlic clove and also lightly brown.
4. Finally, add the diced zucchini and corn.
5. Add the mixture of soymilk, vigorous vegetable broth and soy sauce.
6. The peanut butter (I like it very creamy and add 4 tablespoons), add pepper and chili powder.
7. Cover and simmer everything until the zucchini is done. If it has become too thick, add some soy milk or water.
8. Finally, to taste again.
9. The sauce should be nice creamy with a good spiciness and seasoning.
10. If necessary, add a little broth, salt, chili powder or pepper. If you like it even thicker, you can of course also thicken with some flour.
11. In addition, there is rice for me. If you like, you can also choose the other side dishes.
12. Some fresh parsley provides the last whistle.

330. Bolognese sauce with lots of vegetables

Ingredients

- 2 tbsp   oil
- 1 kg   Minced meat, from beef
- 500 g   Soup vegetables, (carrot, leek, celery)
- 1 Carrot
- 2 Onion
- 2 Garlic cloves)
- 1 small one   Hot peppers, hot
- 50 ml   Red wine, dry
- 800 g   Tomato (s), from the tin, pieced with juice
- 3 tsp   Oregano, dried
- 1/2 tsp Basil, dried
- 1 Bay leaf
- 1 pinch sugar
- 250 ml Beef broth, seasoned
- 2 Teaspoons Salt, approx.
- 1/4 TL Black pepper
- 1 teaspoon Beef broth, instant, approx.

Preparation

1. First, in a separate pan, mince the minced meat in the hot oil until it is crumbly. That takes about 10 minutes. Drain the fat

as best as possible, but leave about 3 tablespoons in the pan. Put the minced meat in the ceramic pot. Now clean the vegetables - carrots, onions, leeks, celery, garlic and hot peppers - as usual and, if possible, grate them roughly in a food processor. The vegetable mixture is then gently cooked in the remaining oil over medium heat. Deglaze with a good shot of red wine (but do not boil) and give everything to the minced meat. Finally, add the spices, the dried herbs and the liquids. Carefully mix and level slightly. Do not be alarmed, the Bolognese seems very plump - but that's the way it should be! The Schmorzeit is approx. 2 hours HIGH and 2 - 3 hours LOW. In between you may also stir. Season with salt, pepper and a little more brewing powder.

2. Serve with spaghetti and sprinkle with grated hard cheese (eg Parmesan).

331. Vegetables - lasagna a la mouSse

Ingredients

- Lasagne plate (s) (without egg - without precooking)
- 1 big one   Onion (s), finely diced
- 2 toe / n   Garlic, finely chopped
- 2 m. -Large   Zucchini, grated
- 2 m. -Large   Carrot (s), grated
- 1 m. -Large   Pepper (s), red, small diced
- 2 pole / s   Celery, in fine slices
- 200 g   Mushrooms, in fine slices
- 400 g   sour cream
- 150 g   Cheese, raw milk Emmentaler, grated
- 1 tbsp   olive oil
- salt and pepper
- chili powder
- 400 g   Herbal cream cheese or light herb cream cheese
- 2 toe / n   Garlic, crushed
- something   water
- 100 g   Parmesan, grated
- Olive oil, for the form

Preparation

1. Heat the olive oil in a large, coated pan (or wok) and fry the onion, garlic and vegetables vigorously for 5 minutes. Remove the pan / wok from the griddle, allow to cool briefly and mix in the sour cream and cheese.
2. Mix the herb cream cheese with the garlic and enough water to make a very creamy sauce.
3. Rub a large casserole dish well with olive oil.
4. First so much cream cheese sauce that the casserole is well covered, then "stratified": a layer of lasagne leaves, cream cheese sauce, a layer of vegetables, a layer of lasagne leaves, cream cheese sauce, vegetables, etc. The last two layers should be lasagna leaves and cream cheese Be sauce.
5. Cover the lasagne with aluminum foil or a lid and leave to soak in the refrigerator for at least 5 hours (better longer, up to 12 hours).
6. Preheat the oven to 180 degrees top / bottom heat.
7. Sprinkle the grated Parmesan cheese over the lasagna and bake for 45 minutes.

332. Fried noodles with vegetables and meat (Asian)

Ingredients

- 200 g   Chinese egg noodles
- 2 liters water
- 1 tbsp   salt
- 2 tbsp   oil
- 200 g   Pork or turkey meat
- 3 Spring onions)
- 1 Pepper
- 2 Carrot
- 1 / 4 liters   Water, hot
- 1 teaspoon   Broth, grained
- 2 tbsp   soy sauce
- 1 tbsp   cornstarch
- salt and pepper
- 2 tbsp   oil
- soy sauce

Preparation

1. Boil the noodles in the boiling salted water according to the packing instructions and strain.
2. Fry the meat in a large pan with oil for 3 minutes.

3. Clean the spring onions wash and cut into 2 cm long pieces. Wash the peppers, cut in half, corer them and cut into strips. Wash the carrots, peel and grate or cut into thin slices.
4. Add the sliced vegetables to the meat in the pan and fry for 2 minutes.
5. Mix the stock, soy sauce and cornstarch well in a bowl, add to the frying pan and add to the rest of the ingredients.
6. Heat the oil in another pan, add the drained noodles and cook for about 3 minutes. Then add the vegetable-meat mixture and mix.
7. Put in a preheated bowl.

333. Salmon with vegetables and potatoes

Ingredients

- 1 Salmon (wild salmon, in whole)
- 6 m. -Large   Potato
- 4 m. -Large   Carrot
- 2 broccoli
- 4 m. -Large   Tomatoes)
- 1 / 4 liters   vegetable stock
- 1 cup   cream
- 2 tbsp   Herbs, French (or of your choice), chopped
- n. B.   Butter, cut into flakes
- n. B.   salt and pepper

preparation

1. Peel the potatoes and carrots. Divide the broccoli into florets. Halve the potatoes and cut the carrots into 3 - 5 cm long pieces.
2. Cook the potatoes and carrots for about 10 minutes and the broccoli in salted water for about 3 minutes. Drain the water and distribute the potatoes and vegetables on the meat pan from the oven. Divide the salmon into about eight portions and place between vegetables and potatoes. Wash the tomatoes, cut crosswise and also put on the tin. Now mix the broth and cream together with the herbs, salt and pepper (Tip:

If you love garlic, you can also add it to the broth). Now pour this broth over the ingredients on the plate and spread butter flakes over the vegetables and salmon as needed.
3. Cook in the preheated oven at 200 ° C circulating air for approx. 30 minutes. Serve hot.
4. The recipe can also be prepared well for a party and - when it's time - simply put it in the oven.

334. Fried salmon on Mediterranean vegetables

Ingredients

- 4 Pepper (s), red, coarsely crushed
- 1 m. -Large   Eggplant (s), roughly minced
- 3 m. -Large   Zucchini, roughly minced
- 1 bunch Vegetable onion (s), roughly chopped
- 750 g   Salmon fillet (s) (TK), thawed, pieced
- 1 Lemon (s), the juice of it
- 1 glass Pesto (basil pesto)
- Flour
- Seasoned Salt
- olive oil
- vegetable stock
- Ketchup (curry ketchup), spicy
- paprika
- pepper
- 1 pinch sugar
- Fat for the mold

Preparation

1. Fry the prepared vegetables in a large pan while stirring with the hot olive oil. Add a little vegetable stock and let it simmer

for about 7-10 minutes with the lid. Season with curry ketchup, herbal salt, paprika, pepper and sugar as needed.
2. In the meantime, marinate the thawed salmon pieces with lemon juice and then season with herb salt. Turn in a little flour and brown on both sides in olive oil.
3. Put the vegetables in a greased casserole dish, arrange the salmon pieces on top and spread generously with the basil pesto.
4. In the preheated oven overcool at 200 ° C convection for about 7-10 minutes.
5. This tastes baguette or flatbread.

335. Oven Chicken With Vegetables

Ingredients

- 4 Chicken legs, fresh or frozen
- 5 Potato
- 5 Carrot
- 2 toe   garlic, roughly chopped
- Onion
- 100 ml olive oil
- 1 teaspoon   Paprika powder, sweet
- 1 teaspoon   Paprika powder, pink
- 1 teaspoon   salt
- 1 teaspoon   thyme
- 3 toe / n Garlic, pressed

Preparation

1. Peel and dice the potatoes and carrots. Peel and halve the onion, finely dice one half and cut the other into rings. Add together with 2 coarsely chopped garlic cloves to the potato and carrot cubes.
2. Then mix a marinade with oil, paprika, salt, thyme and pressed garlic. So that the chicken thighs brush (very important: also marinade under the skin!). Add the rest of the marinade to 1 - 2 teaspoons of the potato and carrot mixture and mix well, season with salt, if necessary.

3. Put the vegetable mixture into a large baking dish, put the chicken thighs on top and bake at 200 ° C for 60 - 70 minutes. Possibly. brush with remaining marinade. After about half of the baking time, I turn the thighs and let them take some color from below for a few minutes. To make the skin crispy, but in any case turn it again a few minutes before the end of cooking time.
4. Vegetables and meat become very fragrant when they are baked together and after the schnippelei the whole thing cooks itself by itself. With certainty the recipe can also be changed with other vegetables (zucchini, paprika, ...) or other spices.

336. Beefsteak with mustard and herb topping and vegetables

Ingredients

- 2 thick Beefsteak (s) (beef steaks), each about 250 g, well-hung
- 3 m. -Large   Carrot
- 2 m. -Large   zucchini
- 2 TL, heaped   Mustard medium hot
- something   herbs of Provence
- something   pepper
- something   Salt (Society Garlic salt) or Himalayan salt
- something   Olive oil or coconut oil
- n. B.   Herbs, fresh (thyme, garlic, mushroom)
- something   Leeks or onions, optional

preparation

1. Rub the two steaks well with olive oil and cover for at least 3 hours in the fridge (better already 1 day before). Half an hour before frying (preferably in an iron pan) take out of the refrigerator. Preheat the oven to 80 ° C without circulating air.
2. Make the pan very hot and fry the steaks without further oil. Fry for 1.5 - 2 (otherwise 3) minutes on each side, depending on the thickness.
3. Sprinkle the steaks with mustard, sprinkle with Provence pepper and herbs, wrap in aluminum foil and place in the

oven. Let rest for 10-15 minutes. The steaks are salted after resting.
4. In the meantime, peel the carrots, wash the zucchini and cut both into small pieces. Fry in a pan with 2 tablespoons of coconut oil (if necessary, sauté onions and leeks) and let it cook. Season with salt, pepper and fresh herbs to taste.

ENTRIES

337. Eggplant and chickpea bites

INGREDIENTS

- 3 large aubergines cut in half (make a few cuts in the flesh with a knife) Spray
- oil
- 2 large cloves garlic, peeled and deglazed
- 2 tbsp. coriander powder
- 2 tbsp. cumin seeds
- 400 g canned chickpeas, rinsed and drained
- 2 Tbsp. chickpea flour
- Zest and juice of 1/2 lemon
- 1/2 lemon quartered for serving
- 3 tbsp. tablespoon of polenta

PREPARATION

1. Heat the oven to 200°C (180°C rotating heat, gas level 6). Spray the eggplant halves generously with oil and place them on the meat side up on a baking sheet. Sprinkle with coriander and cumin seeds, and then place the cloves of garlic on the

plate. Season and roast for 40 minutes until the flesh of eggplant is completely tender. Reserve and let cool a little.

2. Scrape the flesh of the eggplant in a bowl with a spatula and throw the skins in the compost. Thoroughly scrape and make sure to incorporate spices and crushed roasted garlic. Add chickpeas, chickpea flour, zest, and lemon juice. Crush roughly and mix well, check to season. Do not worry if the mixture seems a bit soft - it will firm up in the fridge.

3. Form about twenty pellets and place them on a baking sheet covered with parchment paper. Let stand in the fridge for at least 30 minutes.

4. Preheat oven to 180°C (rotating heat 160°C, gas level 4). Remove the meatballs from the fridge and coat them by rolling them in the polenta. Place them back on the baking sheet and spray a little oil on each. Roast for 20 minutes until golden and crisp. Serve with lemon wedges. You can also serve these dumplings with a spicy yogurt dip with harissa, this delicious but spicy mashed paste of hot peppers and spices from the Maghreb.

338. Baba Ghanouj

INGREDIENTS

- 1 large aubergine, cut in half lengthwise
- 1 head of garlic, unpeeled
- 30 ml (2 tablespoons) of olive oil
- Lemon juice to taste

PREPARATION

1. Put the grill at the center of the oven. Preheat the oven to 350 ° F. Line a baking sheet with parchment paper.
2. Place the eggplant on the plate, skin side up. Roast until the meat is very tender and detaches easily from the skin, about 1 hour depending on the size of the eggplant. Let cool.
3. Meanwhile, cut the tip of the garlic cloves. Place the garlic cloves in a square of aluminum foil. Fold the edges of the sheet and fold together to form a tightly wrapped foil. Roast with the eggplant until tender, about 20 minutes. Let cool. Purée the pods with a garlic press.
4. With a spoon, scoop out the flesh of the eggplant and place it in the bowl of a food processor. Add the garlic puree, the oil, and the lemon juice. Stir until purée is smooth and pepper.
5. Serve with mini pita bread.

339. Mixes of snacks

INGREDIENTS

- 6 c. margarine
- 2 tbsp. Worcestershire sauce
- 1 ½ tbsp. spice salt
- ¾ c. garlic powder
- ½ tsp. onion powder
- 3 cups Crispix
- 3 cups Cheerios
- 3 cups corn flakes
- 1 cup Kix
- 1 cup pretzels
- 1 cup broken bagel chips into 1-inch pieces

PREPARATION

1. Preheat the oven to 250F (120C)
2. Melt the margarine in a large roasting pan. Stir in the seasoning. Gradually add the ingredients remaining by mixing so that the coating is uniform.
3. Cook 1 hour, stirring every 15 minutes. Spread on paper towels to let cool. Store in a tightly-closed container.

340. Herbal Cream Cheese Tartines

INGREDIENTS

- 20 regular round melba crackers
- 1 clove garlic, halved
- 1 cup cream cheese spread
- ¼ cup chopped herbs such as chives, dill, parsley, tarragon or thyme
- 2 tbsp. minced French shallot or onion
- ½ tsp. black pepper
- 2 tbsp. tablespoons water

PREPARATION

1. In a medium-sized bowl, combine the cream cheese, herbs, shallot, pepper, and water with a hand blender.
2. Rub the crackers with the cut side of the garlic clove.
3. Serve the cream cheese with the rusks

341. Spicy crab dip

INGREDIENTS

- 1 can of 8 oz softened cream cheese
- 1 tbsp. to . finely chopped onions
- 1 tbsp. at . lemon juice
- 2 tbsp. at . Worcestershire sauce
- 1/8 tsp. at t. black
- pepper Cayenne pepper to taste
- 2 tbsp. to s. of milk or non-fortified rice drink
- 1 can of 6 oz of crabmeat

PREPARATION

1. Preheat the oven to 375 ° F (190 ° C).
2. Pour the cream cheese into a bowl. Add the onions, lemon juice, Worcestershire sauce, black pepper, and cayenne pepper. Mix well. Stir in the milk/rice drink. Add the crabmeat and mix until you obtain a homogeneous mixture.
3. Pour the mixture into a baking dish. Cook without covering for 15 minutes or until bubbles appear. Serve hot with low-sodium crackers or triangle cut pita bread. OR
4. Microwave until bubbles appear, about 4 minutes, stirring every 1 to 2 minutes.

342. Potatoes" of Parmesan cheese

INGREDIENTS

- 75 g grated Parmesan cheese
- 1 tbsp (8 g) Chia seeds
- 2 tbsp (20 g) whole flaxseeds
- 2½ tbsp (20 g) pumpkin seeds

Instructions

- Preheat the oven to 180 ° C (350 ° F).
- Cover a baking sheet with baking paper.
- Mix the cheese and seeds in a bowl.
- With a spoon, put small piles of the mixture on the baking paper, leaving some space between them. Do not flatten the piles. Bake for 8 to 10 minutes. Check frequently. "Potatoes" should take a light brown color, but not dark brown.
- Remove from the oven and let cool before removing the "potatoes" from the paper and serve them.

343. "Potatoes" cheese keto

INGREDIENTS

- 250 g cheddar cheese or provolone cheese or Edam cheese, grated
- ½ tsp Spanish paprika

INSTRUCTIONS

- Preheat the oven to 200 ° C (400 ° F). Place the slices of cheese on a baking sheet covered in baking paper.
- Sprinkle the ground paprika on top and bake for about 8-10 minutes, depending on the thickness of the cheese slices. Pay attention to the end so that the cheese does not burn: the burned cheese usually has a bitter taste.
- Let cool and enjoy, the "chips" are great as they are, but they are also perfect for serving with guacamole.

344. Low carb halloumi chips, with avocado sauce

INGREDIENTS

- 175 g halloumi cheese
- frying oil *
- Avocado Salsa
- 1 avocado
- 125 ml sour cream or fresh cream
- 1 clove garlic, pressed
- 1 tsp hot sauce or tabasco
- 1 tsp lemon juice
- 1 tbsp (1 g) fresh cilantro, chopped
- salt and ground black pepper

INSTRUCTIONS

- Peel the avocado and remove the bone. Grind roughly with a fork.
- Mix the avocado with the sour cream (or fresh cream) and the rest of the ingredients. Salpimentar to taste and reserve until serving.
- Cut the halloumi lengthwise, into sticks. Clean well with kitchen towels, or they will splash when you put them in the oil.
- Heat the oil up to 180 ° C (350 ° F) in an immersion fryer or pan with high edges. The temperature will be fine if it sizzles

when adding the halloumi. If you use a pan, it is enough to use as much oil as necessary to cover about half the height of the halloumi sticks.
- Fry the sticks for a few minutes on each side. They will be ready when they are golden and crispy on all sides. Spread and enjoy it!

345. Low carb granola bars

INGREDIENTS

- 90 g (150 ml) almonds
- 90 g (225 ml) nuts
- 60 g (100 ml) sesame seeds
- 60 g (100 ml) pumpkin seeds
- 30 g (40 ml) flaxseeds
- 60 g unsweetened grated coconut
- 60 g dark chocolate with a minimum of 70% cocoa solids (for bars)
- 6 tbsp (75 g) coconut oil
- 4 tbsp Tahini (sesame paste)
- 1 tsp vanilla extract
- 2 tsp ground cinnamon
- 1 pinch sea salt
- 2 eggs
- 90 g dark chocolate with a minimum of 70% cocoa solids (to bathe the bars)

INSTRUCTIONS

- Preheat the oven to 175 ° C (350 ° F).
- Mix all the ingredients in a blender or food processor until they are chopped into large pieces.

- Place the mixture in a 7 × 11 roasting pan, preferably lined with baking paper.
- Bake for 15-20 minutes, or until the cake has browned.
- Let cool slightly and remove from the roasting pan. Divide into 20 or 24 portions with a sharp knife.
- Melt the chocolate in a water bath using a double pot or in the microwave oven.
- Bathe each bar in chocolate, but approximately 1.2 cm or on one side only. Let cool completely.
- Store in the refrigerator or freezer.

346. Keto "corn" fritters

INGREDIENTS

- 100 g (225 ml) cauliflower cut into corsages
- 1 medium egg
- ¼ tsp Salt
- 2 tbsp (15 g) coconut flour
- ½ tsp (2 g) granulated erythritol
- 1 tsp anise seeds
- 125 ml (110 g) coconut oil

INSTRUCTIONS

- Grind the cauliflower in the food processor until it has the texture of polenta. Move the cauliflower to a bowl to mix.
- Using a spatula, mix the cauliflower with egg, salt, coconut flour, erythritol and anise.
- Heat the oil in a small skillet (approximately 18 cm [7 "]) at medium temperature (175 ° C [350 ° F]).
- Carefully pour tablespoons of the cauliflower mixture into the oil, do not fry more than 3 at a time.
- Fry until they turn golden brown, turning to cook evenly on both sides (approximately 2½ minutes per side).
- Remove from oil and place on a paper towel to remove excess oil. Serve immediately.

347. Tequeños low in carbohydrates

INGREDIENTS

Tequeños

- 1 medium egg (s)
- 1 tbsp whipping cream
- 100 g (200 ml) ground almonds
- 2 tbsp (15 g) coconut flour
- ½ tsp baking powder
- ½ tsp cream of tartar
- ½ tsp xanthan gum
- 1 tsp butter at room temperature
- 150 g frying cheese

sauce

- ½ ripe avocado (s)
- ½ tsp garlic powder
- ½ lemon, juice
- ½ tsp Salt
- 1 tbsp fresh parsley

INSTRUCTIONS

Tequeños

- Beat the egg and cream together. Reserve.
- Combine almond and coconut flour, add baking powder, cream of tartar and xanthan gum. Mix with a wire whisk until completely mixed.
- Add the butter and pour half of the egg and cream mixture (reserve the rest for later). Mix with a spatula until everything is well combined.
- Work the dough with your hands for half a minute, to turn it into a softball. Wrap it in a plastic film and let it sit at room temperature for 5 minutes.
- Place the ball between two pieces of waxed paper (approximately 30 x 30 cm [12 "by 12"]).
- Press the dough to flatten it, then use a rolling pin to obtain a very thin layer (approximately 3 mm [3/16"] thick). Try to keep the shape as rectangular as possible. Cut into long ribbons: a ribbon for each tequeño (2 per serving).
- Cut the frying cheese into sticks (2 per serving), all the same size (approximately 8 cm [3 "] long.) Squeeze each stick wrapped in a paper towel to remove excess moisture.
- Very carefully, wrap each cheese stick with a dough tape, sealing at the ends. You may need to join the dough again if it breaks somewhere.

- Paint the sticks with the egg and cream mixture that we reserve from the previous steps.
- Bake in a preheated oven at 150 ° C [300 ° F] for 20 minutes, or until they acquire a beautiful light golden brown color. You need to keep an eye on them, since almond flour is a bit unpredictable and can go from golden to burning in a short time.

For the sauce

Combine all ingredients except parsley, and blend using an immersion blender until you get a very smooth creamy consistency. Mix the parsley.

CPSIA information can be obtained
at www.ICGtesting.com
Printed in the USA
BVHW010907311021
620172BV00016B/52